Essentials
of
Family Therapy

A Structured Summary of Nine Approaches

SECOND EDITION

William M. Walsh
University of Northern Colorado

James A. McGraw
Webster University – Kansas City, Missouri

LOVE PUBLISHING COMPANY®
Denver • London • Sydney

Library of Congress Controlled Number: 2002101690

Copyright © 2002, 1996 Love Publishing Company
Printed in the U.S.A.
ISBN 0-89108-297-2
ISBN 978-0-89108-297-2

Contents

3 ■ Bowenian Theory   31

4 ■ Structural Family Therapy   47

5 ■ Strategic Family Therapy   63

6 ■ Milan Model of Family Systems Therapy   81

7 ■ Adlerian Family Therapy   97

8 ■ Solution-Focused Family Therapy   107

11 ■ Descriptive Summary of Nine Additional Approaches   161

Preface

The second edition of *Essentials of Family Therapy* maintains the same primary objective as the first edition: to provide a concise overview of a number of popular systemic approaches to family therapy using a consistent format that enables readers to quickly identify similarities and differences among the models. The intended audience continues to include graduate students in family systems and marriage and family therapy classes, clinicians in practice, and professionals preparing for licensure examinations.

Chapter 1 presents a cursory overview of family therapy models in general and discusses the underlying tenets of systems theory as it applies to family therapy. Each of the next nine chapters addresses a particular family therapy model. The chapters begin with some background information and then move on to historical influences, philosophy, theoretical tenets, perspectives on family function and dysfunction, assessment and diagnosis, goals of treatment, the treatment process, techniques, the roles of the therapist, and an evaluation of the model with regard to application, research support, and other areas. As with the first edition, this second edition does not attempt to supplant the primary sources associated with the models of family therapy that are outlined. For further inquiry, readers are encouraged to review the primary sources listed in the references at the end of each chapter.

Certain changes and updates in the second edition are noteworthy:

- The inclusion of a chapter on narrative family therapy

- An expanded Chapter 1, which includes a brief discussion of first- and second-order cybernetic models and an overview of family therapy outcome research

- Updated information (e.g., recent research findings) on various models of family therapy

- Formatting changes designed to make the chapters more user-friendly, such as the increased use of an outline format and the inclusion at the beginning of each chapter of a list of key terms, which is intended to serve as an advanced organizer for the reader

- The expansion of the final chapter to include descriptions of emotion-focused therapy, multisystemic therapy, and feminist family therapy.

Acknowledgments

We offer thanks to the following individuals for their thoughtfulness and contributions to the preparation of the manuscript for this book:

- Leann Wyrick, M.A., for her many hours of editing and preparation of each chapter

- Erik Sween, Psy.D., for his expert and insightful suggestions for the chapter on narrative family therapy

- Erica Lawrence for her perceptive, knowledgeable, and accurate editing and suggestions for this book

- Colleagues and students who provided personal feedback on their experiences with the first edition

We also recognize and appreciate the support of family members who are friends and friends who are family.

1

A Brief Overview of Family Therapy Models

The theories of family therapy outlined in this book differ from one another in numerous respects, yet to varying degrees they all can be classified as systemic models. Systemic approaches to personality and counseling (also referred to as interpersonal or relational-ecological approaches) are qualitatively different from intrapsychic (also referred to as individual or psychological) approaches, the other model within this classification framework. These two approaches are predicated on different philosophical assumptions and entail divergent ways of conceptualizing and working with human concerns. (See Table 1.1 for key distinctions between these models.)

Making a distinction between these types of approaches is important for several reasons, two of which are described here. First, for many individuals in the helping professions who were initially trained

TABLE 1.1

Key Distinctions Between Intrapsychic and Systemic Models

Intrapsychic Models	Systemic Models
Physical laws apply to human behavior	Physical laws cannot adequately account for complex human interactions
Primacy of linear cause and effect relationships	Circular and reciprocal cause and effect relationships
Objectivity in the therapeutic process	Subjectivity in the therapeutic process
Focus on the individual (e.g., characteristics, traits)	Focus on the system (relationships, patterns)
Quantitative methodology (e.g., true experiment conditions as the preferred mode of research)	Qualitative methodologies (e.g., phenomenological, case study) as acceptable modes of research

in intrapsychic models of psychology, the mental shift to a systemic paradigm can be difficult and confusing (Softas-Nall, Baldo, & Jackson, 1997). Higgins and Dermer (2001) elaborated on this point when they wrote: "When working with couples and families, students are expected to make the difficult transition from thinking in parts and cause and effect (linear thinking) to thinking in terms of wholes, inter-relationships, and circularity (systems thinking)" (p. 182). The transition is facilitated by a clear understanding of the two approaches. Second, without an awareness of the foundation of a theory, a therapist may find it difficult to maintain congruence between a theory and its application in clinical practice. For example, clinicians may assume they are using a systemic approach because several family members are present in a session when in actuality they are working from an intrapsychic model. Conversely, an interpersonal or family systems approach may be utilized even when only one individual is present in the session (Baldwin, 1998). A clear understanding of these approaches helps to alleviate these problems.

This introductory chapter provides an overview of intrapsychic and systemic models, briefly describing the historical origins and philo-sophical foundations of each type of model. Readers are asked to remember that there are overlapping areas between intrapsychic and interpersonal models and that some differences are subject to interpre-tation. The intention of this chapter is twofold: to enable readers to have a clearer and more accurate understanding of the foundations of intrapsychic and systemic models of therapy by contrasting them with each other; and to offer a basic overview of systemic thinking, which provides the foundation for the family therapy models outlined in this book.

The Intrapsychic Paradigm

The intrapsychic paradigm has a long history in the formative years of the discipline of psychology. Some of the early pioneers in the devel-opment of psychotherapy include Sigmund Freud, B. F. Skinner, and Carl Rogers. Their theories of human behavior arose out of their respective cultural and temporal contexts, but all were grounded in a

Western, positivistic belief system that reflected the influence of some of the day's giants in science, including Sir Isaac Newton, René Descartes, and Francis Bacon. The origins of this belief system arose from an examination of the relationships among objects in the physical world (e.g., planetary motion). Key aspects of the Newtonian/Cartesian belief system include objectivity, linear cause and effect relationships, and generalizability. This approach leads to a view of the universe as an immense clockwork; that is infinitely complex yet theoretically understandable and predictable if the laws governing matter and energy are discovered and accurately measured.

Within this Newtonian/Cartesian worldview, a scientific understanding of human behavior is based on the following four assumptions:

1. The laws of nature and human psychological processes are subject to the same laws as are physical bodies.
2. Human behavior and psychological processes can be studied through the scientific method, which entails objective observation (i.e., the assumption that the observer does not influence the observed) and reductionism (i.e., striving toward understanding by breaking things down into their component parts).
3. Mechanistic cause and effect relationships can explain reality and human behavior.
4. Reality can be perceived and measured objectively.

Capra (1983) suggested that the psychoanalytic view of human behavior was closely related to these assumptions of Newtonian mechanics. A metaphor that has been used to describe this paradigm is "humans as machines." Another hallmark of intrapsychic models is that they tend to view individuals (i.e., identified clients) and their internal processes as the seat of pathology and as the object of therapeutic intervention. Early theories of personality and counseling adhered to these tenets of the intrapsychic paradigm to varying degrees. Some theorists asserted that psychology could achieve credibility only by modeling itself rigorously after the physical sciences (e.g., John Watson's view of behaviorism). Other theorists acknowledged that human behavior may be less subject to deterministic laws and may have the capacity to be self-directed (e.g., Carl Roger's person-centered approach).

More recent theories of personality and counseling have extended and revised the initial formulations upon which these models were based while preserving many of the fundamental presuppositions. Numerous authors have detailed the historical and philosophical basis of the intrapsychic paradigm of psychology. A particularly useful book to review for an in-depth inquiry is *Human Change Processes* (Mahoney, 1991).

The following quote by Abraham Maslow (1966) provides a critique of the intrapsychic model and a transition to the systemic model:

> The search for a fundamental datum (in psychology) is itself a refection of a whole world-view, a scientific philosophy which assumes an atomistic world—a world in which complex things are built out of simple elements. The first task of such a scientist then is to reduce the so-called complex to the so-called simple. This is done by analysis, by finer and finer separating until we come to the irreducible. This task has succeeded well enough elsewhere in science, for a time at least. In psychology it has not." (p. 3–4)

The Systemic Paradigm

Although the systemic model arose relatively recently in Western thought, throughout history various cultures have espoused ideas compatible with systemic thinking. A systemic worldview has a long tradition in various belief systems such as Taoism and Buddhism. Ludwig von Bertalanffy (1968) identified Western philosophers Hegel and Marx as historical predecessors of general systems theory.

As noted earlier, systemic models of family therapy are based on different philosophical assumptions than are intrapsychic models. Systemic models focus on the primacy of the family system in understanding individuals' behaviors. A working understanding of the systemic paradigm is essential to fully comprehend these models. Common tenets of systemic models of family therapy include the following:

- The whole is greater than the sum of its constituent parts (a premise that contrasts with the reductionist approach of the intrapsychic paradigm). In the systemic view, components of a system (i.e., individuals in a family) can be understood only within the context of the whole system. These individuals relate to one another in some consistent fashion, and the system is structured by these relationships (Goldenberg & Goldenberg, 1991). Because human behavior arises within a social system, it can be understood only within this context.

- Boundaries define the borders that separate a family system from other systems (e.g., other families, cultures, environmental systems), making the family a distinct entity.

- Attributions of linear cause and effect are replaced by notions of circular, simultaneous, and reciprocal cause and effect.

- A change in one part of a social system (e.g., an individual family member) affects all other parts of that system (e.g., the entire family).

- Systems tend to be self-regulating; that is, systems tend to exist in a relatively steady state for substantial periods of time. The tendency in a system is to seek homeostasis or equilibrium. This balance-seeking function serves to maintain stability and sometimes prevents change.

- When a family system is out of equilibrium, feedback mechanisms attempt to bring the family back to the status quo. Feedback is defined as the return of a portion of the output of a system back into the system (Nichols & Schwartz, 1991). The feedback serves to control the system by providing an inherent regulatory function. For example, if a child attempts to assume a parental role with an older sibling, feedback from the system (e.g., nasty looks from other family members) will serve to discourage the "deviant" behavior and return the interpersonal relations back to a state of equilibrium. Feedback also can provide the impetus for change within a system.

- The methods used to restore equilibrium (e.g., a child acting out to foster parental cooperation) can become problems themselves and are sometimes termed homeostatic mechanisms.

- The quantity and direction of energy in a system have an impact on the organization and functioning of that system. Entropy describes the tendency of a system to move into disorder. It brings disorganization, and an undifferentiated form of the system (e.g., family chaos) may result (Bateson, 1972). Negentropy describes the tendency of a system to be flexible and open to new experience and to change or discard interaction patterns that are no longer usable (Kantor & Lehr, 1975). Both of these energy sources act on systems.

■ Conceptualizations and interventions from a family systems perspective focus on relationships within the entire family system rather than focusing on one individual in the family (i.e., the "identified patient").

■ Systemic models espouse equifinality, the concept that there are multiple causes for any behavior or event and multiple effects flowing from any behavior or event. This concept also suggests the tendency of a system to reach the same final state using various methods and from different initial conditions (Goldenberg & Goldenberg, 1985).

All theories of human behavior are a function of the cultural and temporal context in which they are embedded. The evolution of a systemic approach to family therapy exemplifies this position in that systemic thinking is compatible with modern developments in physics (e.g., the nonexistence of objective, detached observation; questioning of linear cause and effect conceptualizations; and the interconnectedness of all phenomena, whether they relate to individuals in a family or subatomic particles). Interestingly, intrapsychic models followed the lead of Newtonian physics while systemic models of family therapy resonate with the physics of quantum mechanics and relativity theory.

Seminal thinkers in the development of family systems theory such as Gregory Bateson, Murray Bowen, Salvador Minuchin, and Jay Haley have added their own formulations to this mode of thinking; therefore, their theories differ on some specifics of family function and clinical practice. Theorists and practitioners in the interpersonal or systemic camp also differ with regard to the degree to which they hold to a systemic paradigm. For example, Jay Haley typically is seen as a systems purist whereas Virginia Satir's model combines elements of an intrapsychic perspective with a systemic paradigm. More recent family theorists such as William Walsh (1980) have developed integrative models of family therapy that combine intrapsychic and interpersonal elements into a theoretically coherent and consistent structure.

Within the systemic paradigm of family therapy, models are sometimes categorized as first-generation models (e.g., communication/validation, Bowenian, structural), second-generation models (e.g., strategic, Milan, and integrative), or third-generation models (e.g., solution focused and narrative). This categorization refers to the chronological order of these models and to the progression of concepts within these models. A sampling of relevant concepts that continue to evolve in family therapy include the idea of a universal family structure, the role of the therapist, and the nature of the therapeutic process. These concepts serve as characteristics by which distinctions are made among the three generations of family therapy models, and some distinctions appear to be in the eye of the beholder. Examples of different perspectives on these types of issues have been documented in the professional literature. Discourses between Minuchin (1998), Combs and Freedman (1998), Tomm (1998), and Sluzki (1998), as documented in the *Journal of Marital and Family Therapy* (e.g., "Where Is the Family in Narrative Family Therapy?" by Minuchin, 1998; "Tellings and Retellings," by Combs and Freedman, 1998), portray the value and richness of these discussions.

A Caveat to Remember

It is critical to remember that there is no purely correct worldview. Because intrapsychic and systemic models are based on assumptions, neither paradigm is right or wrong. Both intrapsychic and systemic models are useful in the appropriate context and with the appropriate level of intervention. In addition, both paradigms have contributed to our understanding of and ability to intervene in human behavior.

Research in Marriage and Family Therapy

Recent emphasis on examining research outcomes of marriage and family therapy (MFT) has resulted in reviews of the literature and meta-analyses of relevant studies. This body of knowledge provides tentative support for the following general claims about MFT:

■ MFT appears to be effective, as evidenced by clinical trial research, in which an MFT group demonstrated better outcomes than a no-treatment control group, and meta-analytic studies (Sexton & Alexander, 1999).

■ For many presenting concerns, the effect size for MFT is comparable to that for individual therapy approaches (Shadish, Ragsdale, Glaser, & Montgomery, 1995).

■ MFT has been utilized with diverse populations exhibiting a wide variety of presenting concerns (Pinsof & Wynne, 1995).

■ Some studies suggest that MFT may have better outcomes than group, individual, or psychoeducational treatments for particular problems, such as substance abuse (Stanton & Shadish, 1997).

■ A study by Henggler, Melton, Smith, Schoenwald, and Handley (1993) demonstrated greater cost-effectiveness for family-based interventions than for conventional treatment for delinquency.

■ When the potential methodological confounds in the research are factored in, no particular model of MFT appears to produce better outcomes than any other (Shadish et al., 1995).

■ Therapeutic outcomes for serious disorders tend to be better when family intervention is provided as an adjunct to conventional treatment (e.g., medication, psychoeducation, individual therapy) (Baldwin & Huggins, 1997).

These findings should be considered cautiously because of the complexity of the research problems associated with marital and family therapy, including issues related to sampling, measuring dependent variables, and standardizing treatment across studies. In addition, because some of the research that has been included in meta-analyses of MFT has used approaches (e.g., behavioral family therapy) that are not systemic in theory or application, the generalizability of the findings to systemic models must be considered. And because some systemic models eschew research based on quantitative methods (e.g., the need for rigorous control, researcher objectivity, and the generalizability of findings), qualitative research approaches (e.g., case studies) may be more highly valued by proponents of these models.

Despite the aforementioned concerns about the research in MFT, numerous scientific articles have acknowledged the improvements that have occurred in the research methods and have noted that the credibility of the approaches has been enhanced (Baldwin & Huggins, 1997; Pinsof & Wynne, 1995). At the same time, the literature also calls for improved quality of research methods to provide additional support for the effectiveness of these approaches. For a more in-depth review of the research literature, readers are encouraged to read the research articles previously cited.

In addition to studies that have looked at the differences among MFT models, research has been conducted examining the common factors that promote change. Sprenkle, Blow, and Dickey (1999) asserted that the common factors that account for most of the variance associated with outcome include client variables, therapeutic alliance, and client expectancy. In other words, the differences among models seem irrelevant with regard to client outcome. Sprenkle et al. noted, "There is not a scintilla of evidence for the general superiority of 'unique' models" (p. 353). The authors posited that certain aspects of MFT models may offer advantages over individual approaches (e.g., family models engage multiple family members simultaneously and privilege clients' stories). They added, however, that these claims need to be validated through research.

The weight of evidence suggests that MFT is effective across a wide array of presenting concerns. When delving into more specific research questions—such as, "Which approach is most effective with which presenting concerns and using what outcome measures?"—drawing conclusions from existing research becomes more difficult and provisional. While each of the remaining chapters of this book presents a cursory description of research findings germane to a particular model, in general there is a paucity of research that examines the effectiveness of individual models (Naden, Rasmussen, Morrissette, & Johns, 1997).

Regardless of their worldview or choice of model, therapists must remain aware of the model from which they operate (including its assumptions, applications, limitations, and relevant research findings) so that their conceptualizations and interventions remain theoretically consistent. In the article "Families and Family Psychology at the Millennium: Intersecting Crossroads," Kaslow (2001) provided the following perspective on trends that impact families and family therapists around the world. Discussing the continually increasing stresses that families today endure, including changes in traditional family structure, addictions, increased domestic violence, and high rates of divorce, Kaslow (2001) asserted that family therapists are particularly well qualified to assume a leadership role in addressing these concerns.

References

Baldwin, C. (1998). Family systems and the single client. *Family Journal, 5,* 254–256.

Baldwin, C., & Huggins, D. (1997). Marital and family therapy research: Outcomes and implications for practice. *Family Journal, 5,* 212–222.

Bateson, G. (1972). *Steps to an ecology of mind.* New York: Chandler.

Capra, F. (1983). *The turning point: Science, society, and the rising culture.* Toronto: Bantam Books.

Combs, G., & Freedman, J. (1998). Tellings and retellings. *Journal of Marital and Family Therapy, 24,* 405–408.

Goldenberg, I., & Goldenberg, H. (1985). *Family therapy: An overview.* (2nd ed.). Pacific Grove: Brooks/Cole.

Goldenberg, I., & Goldenberg, H. (1991). *Family therapy: An overview.* Pacific Grove, CA: Brooks/Cole.

Henggeler, S. W., Melton, G. B., Smith, L. A. Schoenwald, S. K., & Hanley, J. H. (1993). Family preservation using multisystemic treatment: Long-term follow-up to a clinical trial with serious juvenile offenders. *Journal of Child and Family Studies, 2,* 283–293.

Higgins, J. A., & Dermer, S. (2001). The

use of film in marriage and family counselor education. *Counselor Education & Supervision, 40,* 182–191.

Kantor, D., & Lehr, W. (1975). *Inside the family.* San Francisco: Jossey-Bass.

Kaslow, F. W. (2001). Families and family psychology at the millennium: Intersecting crossroads. *American Psychologist, 56,* 37–46.

Mahoney, M. (1991). *Human change processes: The scientific foundations of psychotherapy.* New York: Basic Books.

Maslow, A. (1966). *The psychology of science.* New York: Harper & Row.

Minuchin, S. (1998). Where is the family in narrative family therapy? *Journal of Marital and Family Therapy, 24,* 397–403.

Naden, M., Rasmussen, K., Morrissette, P., & Johns, K. (1997). Sources of influence and topic areas in family therapy: Trends in three major journals. *Journal of Marital and Family Therapy, 23,* 389–398.

Nichols, M., & Schwartz, R. (1991). *Family therapy: Concepts and methods* (2nd ed.). Boston: Allyn and Bacon.

Pinsof, W. M., & Wynne, L. C. (1995). The efficacy of marital and family therapy: An empirical overview, conclusions, and recommendations. *Journal of Marital and Family Therapy, 21,* 585–613.

Sexton, T. L., & Alexander, J. F. (1999). Family-based empirically supported intervention programs. *Family Digest, 12*(2), 1–14.

Shadish, W. R., Ragsdale, K., Glaser, R.

R., & Montgomery, L. M. (1995). The efficacy and effectiveness of marital and family therapy: A perspective from meta-analysis. *Journal of Marital and Family Therapy, 21,* 345–360.

Sluzki, C. E. (1998). In search of the lost family: A footnote to Minuchin's essay. *Journal of Marital and Family Therapy, 24,* 415–417.

Softas-Nall, B. C., Baldo, T. D., & Jackson, S. M. (1997). Facilitating the transition from individual sessions to systemic family sessions: Issues of supervision and training. *Family Journal, 5,* 257–262.

Sprenkle, D. H., Blow, A. J., & Dickey, M. H. (1999). Common factors and other nontechnique variables in marriage and family therapy. In M. Hubble, B. Duncan, & S. Miller (Eds.), *The heart and soul of change: What works in therapy* (pp. 329–359). Washington, DC: American Psychological Association.

Stanton, M. D., & Shadish, W. R. (1997). Outcome, attrition, and family-couples treatment for drug abuse: A meta-analysis and review of the controlled, comparative studies. *Psychological Bulletin 122:* 170–190.

Tomm, K. (1998). A question of perspective. *Journal of Marital and Family Therapy, 24,* 409–413.

von Bertalanffy, L. (1968). *General systems theory.* New York: Braziller.

Walsh, W. (1980). *A primer in family therapy.* Springfield, IL: Charles C. Thomas.

2

Communication/ Validation Family Therapy

MAJOR THEORIST: Virginia Satir

Key Terms:

Anchoring
Congruent communication
Denominalization
Drama
Family roles
Family sculpting
Human mandala
Noncongruent communication

The essence of Virginia Satir's work lies in enhancing the self-esteem of individuals in a family while concomitantly effecting change in the interpersonal system. The model of family therapy developed by Satir has been known by several names throughout its evolution: conjoint family therapy, process therapy, human validation process model, and, most recently, communication/validation family therapy. It is considered a seminal, or first-generation, model that is typically associated with various approaches under the communication as well as the experiential family therapy classification.

Virginia Satir was raised on a farm in Wisconsin. At an early age she decided to be a detective of parents. The following passage provides insight into how Satir's personality and early development presaged some basic themes in her professional work:

> When I was 5, I decided to become a children's detective on parents. There was so much that went on between my parents that made little or no sense to me. Making sense of things around me, feeling loved, and being competent were my paramount concerns. I did feel loved, and felt I was competent, but making sense of all the contradictions, deletions, and distortions I observed both in my parents' relationship and among people outside in the world was heart-rending and confusion-making to me. Sometimes this situation raised questions about my being loved, but mostly it affected my ability to predict, to see clearly, and to develop my total being. (Satir, 1982, pp. 13–14)

After earning a bachelor's degree at the University of Wisconsin, Satir began her professional career as a teacher. She subsequently earned a master's degree in psychiatric social work from the University of Chicago and began a private practice in Chicago in 1951. This private practice was the beginning of Satir's pioneering work with families. In 1955, Satir began to conceptualize her clinical experience into theory while teaching family therapy at the Illinois State Psychiatric Institute.

Prior to her death in 1988, Satir had devoted much of her professional life to private practice, writing, teaching, and international relations. Known for her personal charisma and her unshakable belief in people, Satir is widely acclaimed as one of the pioneers in family therapy. The work of Virginia Satir continues to be promoted by the Avanta Network, an association composed of human service providers who trained and worked in Satir's model (Horne, 2000).

Historical Influences

Evidence of early training in Freudian psychoanalysis is apparent in Satir's model, although she rejected the essence of deterministic Freudian thought. Also, reviewers have noted similarities between Satir's model, Adler's holistic orientation, and Jung's position on the possibility of personality integration (Satir & Bitter, 1991). Parallels between Satir and Carl Rogers include the belief in the inherent goodness and growth tendency in humans, the importance of self-worth, and an emphasis on congruence. The systemic aspect of Satir's theory was most directly influenced by individuals in the Palo Alto group, particularly Gregory Bateson and Don Jackson. Satir cofounded the Mental Research Institute in Palo Alto with Jules Riskin.

Satir's willingness to explore new ideas led to a cross-fertilization of approaches, which is evident in her model. Her involvement with the Esalen Institute beginning in 1963 allowed for exposure to a wide range of ideas. Indeed, Satir (1982) acknowledged the influence of a diverse group of individuals on her theory and therapeutic style. Among those who influenced Satir's work were Fritz Perls (Gestalt therapy), Eric Berne (transactional analysis), J. L. Moreno (psychodrama), Robert Assigioli (psychosynthesis), George Downing (body therapies), Ida Rolf (life-posturing reintegration), Alex Lowen (bioenergetics), and Milton Erickson (hypnosis).

Philosophy

The basic philosophy underlying the communication/validation family therapy model begins with the idea that humans have an innate growth tendency. All behavior is oriented toward growth "no matter how distorted [behavior] may look" (Satir, 1983, p. 24). Satir conceptualized the self as the core of the "human mandala" and saw individual growth and access to life experience as occurring through the eight aspects of the mandala: physical body, intellect, emotions, the five senses, social needs, nutritional needs, life space needs, and spiritual needs. Satir also embraced a holistic view of humans that emphasized the interaction of the body, mind, and feelings. In Satir and Bitter (1991), Satir noted:

> Once I began to get inklings that the body, mind, and feelings formed a triad, I began to see that if what one feels is not matched by what one says, the body responds as if it has been attacked. The result is physical dysfunction accompanied by either disturbances of emotion or thought. (p. 20)

When, as in Satir's model, humans and the social and organizational systems of which they are a part are viewed as holistic systems, components of the system can be conceptualized as continually interacting to form a dynamic whole. Other characteristics of a systems perspective also apply to Satir's model.

These characteristics include two other components basic to Satir's philosophy. First, rules have an impact on the effectiveness of family functioning by influencing roles, communication processes, and responses to stress. And second, an awareness of experience in the here and now allows for growth to occur in individual and family systems.

Theoretical Tenets

- *Self-esteem:* A core concept in Satir's model, self-esteem refers to the meaning and value people associate with the whole of their personal mandala.

  □ *Individual self-esteem* affects both individual behavior and the interactions among members of a system. A correlation exists between self-esteem and communication (e.g., low self-esteem is associated with poor communication).

☐ *Family self-esteem* affects the way an individual feels about his or her involvement in the system.

■ *Communication:* Satir considers communication to be a major factor influencing relationships with others and ourselves. The way in which we communicate (send and receive information) is learned and can be unlearned. As stated in Satir and Bitter (1991, p. 42), "Communication and self-worth are the foundation of the family system."

☐ *Congruent communication* is straight, direct communication on both verbal and nonverbal levels. The communication or message that is being conveyed is equal to the feelings or emotions that are being felt by the communicant. Congruence involves using words that accurately match personal feelings and experience so that communication and meta-communication match and there are no double-bind messages. A congruent person is alert, balanced, and in touch with personal resources.

☐ *Noncongruent communication* is distorted, incomplete communication involving assumptions or ambiguous double messages. The communication that is being conveyed is not equal to the feelings or emotions that are being felt by the communicant. Conflicting internal feelings often arise as a result. Incongruence denotes the antithesis of congruence. Incongruence is concomitant with distress and dysfunction in the individual and the family system. Examples of incongruent communication patterns include *incomplete communication,* which occurs when a family member makes a statement that lacks details and may cause confusion or assumptions on the part of other members, *assumptions,* which occur when misinterpretation of meaning in the communication of others, *ambiguous communication,* which is mixed messages sent by one member that causes other members to make incorrect or inaccurate judgement regarding members' feelings, and *double messages,* which occur when information conveyed by one family member can have several meanings for the other members, resulting in unclear communication and confusion over intentions.

■ *Roles of Family Members:* Satir's model distinguishes five roles that family members take, each of which is characterized by a particular style of communication.

  □ *The blamer* engages in fault-finding, name-calling, and criticism.
  □ *The placator* engages in apologetic, tentative, and self-effacing communication that is designed to please others.
  □ *The computer* engages in extreme intellectualizing with a paucity of affective content. (This role is also termed the rational role.)
  □ *The distractor* frequently produces irrelevant verbalizations that serve to focus attention away from the issue at hand. (This role is also termed the irrelevant role.)
  □ *The leveler* engages in honest, direct, clear communication with affect that is congruent with the content of the message. (This role is also termed the congruent role.) The leveler style of communication is most effective, and facilitating movement toward this type of communication is a significant aspect of Satir's model.

■ *Rules of the Family:* According to this model, family members develop unwritten rules that govern the daily functioning of the family. The rules may vary depending upon the family members and their relationships. The dynamics of the rules are also influenced by the roles of the members involved and fall into one of two categories:

  □ *Rigid rules:* An example of this might be that a mother has frequent arguments with her son over cleaning his room. This mother may be more rigid in her expectations of her son due to the conflicts that arise. Whereas, her daughter, with whom she seldom argues, may have looser rules in terms of household chores.
  □ *Flexible rules:* In the example above, the daughter and mother have looser or more flexible rules between them. This may create animosity between the siblings or among the family members.

Exploring the rigidity or flexibility of the members in a given family can give the therapist valuable information about the communication and emotional closeness of the family.

Perspectives on
Family Function and Dysfunction

In *Conjoint Family Therapy* (1983), Satir noted that families are held together by seven mutually reinforcing functions:

1. To provide a sexual experience for the mates
2. To contribute to the continuity of the race by producing and nurturing children
3. To cooperate economically by dividing labor between the adults according to gender, convenience, and precedents, and between adults and children according to the child's age and gender
4. To maintain a boundary (by the incest taboo) between the generations so that smooth task-functioning and stable relationships can be maintained
5. To transmit culture to the children by parental teaching
6. To recognize when one of the members is no longer a child but has become an adult capable of performing adult roles and functions
7. To provide for the eventual care of parents by their children

Among these functions, transmission of culture is perhaps the most complex. Parents teach children roles, or socially accepted ways to act with others in different social situations, and these roles vary according to the age and gender of the child. Parents also teach children how to cope with the inanimate environment, how to communicate, how to use words and gestures so that they will have a generally accepted meaning for others, and how and when to express emotions, generally guiding the children's emotional reactivity. The family teaches the child by appealing to his or her love and fear and by communicating to the child verbally, nonverbally, and by example.

In functional families, all of these functions are fulfilled through clear communication in the family system, effective roles, and the implementation of family rules that are few in number, reasonable, relevant, flexible, and consistently applied. Satir and Bitter (1991) provided this description of a functional family:

> Functional family process and personal maturation are characterized by many of the same aspects: an openness to change, flexibility

> of response, the generation of personal choices or system option, an awareness of resources, and appreciation for difference as well as similarity, equality in relationships, personal responsibility, reasonable risk, freedom of experience and expression, clarity, and congruent communication. (p. 25)

This description of a functional family is compatible with Satir's depiction of an "open system"—a clear interchange of information and resources within and without the system that is adaptive and dynamic. The functional family system will operate effectively within the context of larger systems (e.g., social, cultural).

A dysfunctional family has characteristics of a "closed system"—poor interchange of information and resources within and without the system that is maladaptive and rigid. The presence of dysfunction (or "pain," as Satir prefers to call it) in one family member is symptomatic of dysfunction in one of the larger systems, usually the family. Because all families have problems, the difficulties themselves and the ensuing stress are not the "problem"; coping is the problem. Dysfunctional family systems are unable to cope effectively because they have rules that are fixed, arbitrary, and inconsistently applied. These rules tend to maintain the status quo and may serve to bolster parent self-esteem. Ultimately, a dysfunctional system loses its ability to cope and can become chaotic. A depiction of this type of process was provided by Walsh (1980):

> The sequence begins with an incident between family members or between the family and the outside world. This incident causes stress in the unit and unbalances the delicate homeostasis that exists. Some resolution of the incident must be achieved in order to lower the stress and balance the system. A healthy family will use good communication methods in order to achieve a functional resolution of the conflict. An unhealthy family, lacking effective communication methods, will not resolve the incident in a functional way. Lacking this resolution they must then transmit the stress to the identified patient [IP]. This individual will eventually develop symptoms, and he will carry the dysfunction for the entire family. The crucial point in this sequence of events is the attempted resolution of a problem using either good or faulty communication methods. Faulty methods lead directly to

dysfunction, which is expressed in the IP. Therefore, the remediation of individual problem behavior is focused entirely on the family communication process. (p. 12)

Figure 2.1 provides a visual depiction of the process that produces a dysfunctional system.

Assessment and Diagnosis

Assessment occurs simultaneously with therapy. Symptoms that bring families into therapy are always framed within a relational perspective. As noted by Satir (1982), "any symptom signals a blockage in growth and has a survival connection to a system which requires blockage and distortion of growth in some form in all of its members to keep its balance" (p. 12).

Entering into the family process is the first step in assessment. Gathering information about the family directly by asking questions or by observing the dynamics of the family is an overriding concern in the assessment process. Defining the major triadic relationships in the system and uncovering the roles, rules, and communication processes in the family are also key elements of family diagnosis. Examining the relationship messages (which are frequently communicated nonverbally and at a low level of conscious awareness) as well as the content component of communication within a family in the here and now of a session is of paramount importance.

Although Satir did not specify a standard procedure for assessing families, some of the interventions described in the techniques section of this chapter further the assessment process (e.g., family life fact chronology, family map, and sculptures).

Goals of Treatment

The outcome of family therapy employing the communication/validation model in general terms was stated quite clearly by Satir (1983) as follows:

Treatment is completed:
- When family members can complete transactions, check, and ask for feedback.

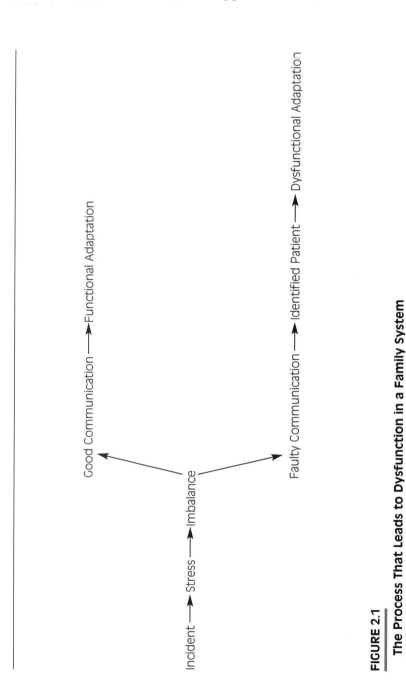

FIGURE 2.1

The Process That Leads to Dysfunction in a Family System

- When they can interpret hostility.
- When they can see how others see them.
- When one member can tell another how he/she manifests him/herself.
- When one member can tell another what he/she hopes, fears, and expects from him/her.
- When they can disagree.
- When they can make choices.
- When they can learn through practice.
- When they can free themselves from harmful effects of past models.
- When they can give a clear message, that is, be congruent in their behavior, with a minimum of difference between feelings and communication, and with a minimum of hidden messages. (p. 176)

Satir and Baldwin (1983) discussed the process of goal attainment in communication/validation family therapy. The first goal is to instill hope and encouragement in family members. The second goal is to access, enhance, and create coping skills. The third goal is to facilitate growth-oriented movement in the family beyond simple symptom relief by releasing and directing energy that was previously tied up in symptomatic behaviors.

In short, the general goal of family therapy in this model is to facilitate growth in the family and between its members in terms of self-esteem and effective communication. Other goals of family therapy could involve movement toward the specific desired changes particular to each unique family.

Treatment Process

The treatment process in the communication/validation model is consistent with the goals of treatment in that family work is a process of facilitating effective communication in a rational context. Five common stages of the treatment process are usually followed regardless of the specific presenting issues:

1. Establish trust with the family. The therapist develops an assessment and treatment plan early to gain the confidence of the family.

2. Develop awareness through experience. The therapist helps the family develop new awarenesses about their functioning by asking specific questions or using specific techniques (see techniques section).
3. Create new understandings in family members through the new or increased awareness of their family dynamics.
4. Have family members express and apply these new understandings through different behaviors during the session.
5. Have family members use the new behaviors outside the therapeutic environment.

Satir and Bitter (1991) noted that with each successful cycle of the change process, the family feels less anxious and movement through the stages becomes easier. Eventually the family may come to see change as an expected part of life.

Techniques

The family therapist is an integral part of the process of facilitating a family's growth in therapy. Consequently, the therapist must be grounded in his or her skills, experiences, and sense of well-being when using these techniques with a family. Many of Satir's interventions arose spontaneously out of her observations and intuitions regarding families in the therapeutic moment. The following 12 techniques are common in communication/validation therapy sessions.

- *Family Sculpting:* A family member (or therapist), acting as "director," physically arranges the members of the family to represent the person's symbolic view of family relationships (Goldenberg & Goldenberg, 1991). All entities that affect the family dynamics (including pets, extended family, friends) are symbolically brought into the sculpture through the use of role playing and fantasy (Satir & Bitter, 1991).

- *Family Maps:* Visual representations, similar to genograms, are created of family structure over three generations. In Satir's use of this technique, three family maps are drawn: mother's family of origin, father's family of origin, and the current family.

- *Ropes:* The binds and pulls of ropes are used in the session to provide concrete representations of the dynamics in the family system.

- *Family Life Fact Chronology:* A holistic family history is made extending from the birth of the oldest grandparents to the present.

- *Drama:* Family members enact significant events in the family's history, providing an opportunity for new perspective and greater insight.

- *Family Reconstruction:* Similar to the use of drama, family reconstruction involves the enactment of events from the family history based on information derived from the family life fact chronology or family maps.

- *Reframing:* The therapist offers a reinterpretation of a situation to create a shift in the perceptions of family members. As noted by Satir (1983), "the therapist decreases threat of blame by accentuating the idea of puzzlement and the idea of good intentions" (p. 142).

- *Humor:* Humor can be used to promote contact between the therapist and family as well as among family members, to mitigate intensity, to clarify or exaggerate a dynamic, and to encourage movement in a way that decreases defensive reactions.

- *Verbalizing Presuppositions:* The therapist overtly states presuppositions that are evident in a family's behavior. For example, Satir would verbalize the hope and expectation for change that a family manifests by virtue of the family's involvement in therapy.

- *Denominalization:* The therapist has a family member provide specific behavioral descriptions for words such as love and respect and discovers exactly what must be done for the person to perceive that he or she is receiving the behavior that is defined. The clarified answer often is related to the individual's primary sensory-based representational system (i.e., visual, auditory, or kinesthetic) (Woods & Martin, 1984).

■ *Anchoring:* The therapist helps family members learn to associate a specific stimulus (or response) with the response it predictably triggers (Dilts & Green, 1982). This technique serves to bring feelings to the level of interpersonal physical experience. Woods and Martin (1984) provided an example of how Satir might have used this technique with a marital couple:

> Satir might ask her to look at her husband and "feel what she feels." When a positive response becomes evident in the individual (i.e., altered breathing, tear), Satir would touch her shoulder gently at the peak of positive emotion. Apparently this helps connect the particular emotion with the touch which makes the feeling more concrete for the individual. (p. 10)

■ *Multiple Family Therapy:* With this technique, numerous unrelated families are brought together for joint family sessions. This technique is also called *group family therapy.*

Role of the Therapist

The primary role of the therapist in the communication/validation model is to guide the family through the process of change. Given this, the therapist should do the following:

■ Create a comfortable, threat-free environment in the sessions such that families can take the risk of looking at their behavior

■ Structure the therapeutic process and set the rules for interaction to decrease threat and create a safe therapeutic environment

■ Allay individual and family defenses by interpreting anger as hurt or by explaining that pain is an acceptable and expressible feeling in therapy

■ Educate clients about their roles to increase self-control and accountability

- Complete gaps or interpret communication, particularly when incongruence exists between the content and the relationship messages (e.g., acknowledging a person's tense body language even though the person says he or she has no anger toward another family member)

- Model effective communication, especially personal congruence

Even more crucial than this list of "shoulds" for therapists is the therapist's self, which Satir asserts is of primary importance in the change process. As noted in Satir and Bitter (1991):

> In this role, the therapist's personhood and humanness [are] more important than any particular set of skills. Faith in the ability of people and in systems to grow and change is essential. (p. 29)

Satir's presence in therapy sessions in the role of therapist is legendary. She was particularly known for her warmth, personal power, and frequent use of touch and activity.

Evaluation of the Communication/Validation Model

As with many other models of family therapy, the efficacy of the communication/validation model has been evaluated primarily on the basis of clinical experience. Satir herself saw more than 5,000 families during her career and reported high rates of success. Research findings relevant to Satir's model include the following studies.

The Family Research Project (Winter, 1989) examined the effectiveness of therapists using the models of Satir, Bowen, and Haley. For the therapists using the Satir model, 57 of 59 families completed therapy (97%). The researchers found that multiple measures of effectiveness of therapy and family change supported the efficacy of the communication/validation model. The study also revealed that families treated in multiple family groups tended to improve more than families seen only as a family unit.

Indirect support for the clinical efficacy of the communication/validation model was provided by Gurman and Kniskern (1986). In their review of the literature on family therapy outcome research, they concluded that:

> the only treatment ingredients that have received consistently positive empirical support as facilitating the outcomes of marital therapies apparently regardless of the general mode of such therapies (cf. Gurman, 1975; Jacobson, 1979) are those that increase couples' communication skills (Birchler, 1979; Gurman & Kniskern, 1977, 1978; Jacobson, 1978, 1979). In fact, at this point, it is defensible to argue that increased communication skills, however they are achieved, are a sine qua non of effective marital therapy. (p. 749)

Gurman and Kniskern (1986) cautioned that this finding should not be construed as stating that improved communication is sufficient for positive outcomes in most cases. Nevertheless, the finding bodes well for the model in light of Satir's emphasis on facilitating clear, congruent communication within the family.

Cottone (1992) called Satir's theory "theoretically deficient" (p. 209), basing this criticism on his position that Satir was unsuccessful in her attempt to integrate intrapsychic and interpersonal concepts into a theoretically consistent model. Despite this criticism, Cottone acknowledged the major contribution Satir made to the field of family therapy.

Recent support for the efficacy of the Satir model was provided by Sprenkle, Blow, and Dickey (1999). In their review of the literature, they asserted that the primary factors that promote positive therapeutic outcome include therapist empathy and a positive therapeutic alliance. Because these factors are integral to the communication/validation model, indirect support regarding the model's efficacy can be inferred.

Another testimony to the impact of Satir's contribution to family therapy is the ongoing work of Avanta, The Virginia Satir Network. Founded in 1977, this not-for-profit organization, which is also referred to as the Avanta Network, operates centers throughout the world that provide services to individuals, families, and therapists (e.g., conferences, workshops, resources) in a manner consistent with Satir's model. Further information about the Avanta Network can be obtained by accessing the Avanta website: http://www.avanta.net.

References

Andreas, S. (1991). *Virgina Satir: The patterns of her magic*. Palo Alto, CA: Science and Behavior Books.

Cottone, R. R. (1992). *Theories and paradigms of counseling and psychotherapy*. Boston: Allyn & Bacon.

Dilts, R., & Green, J. D. (1982). Applications of neurolinguistic programming in family therapy. In A. M. Horne & M. M. Ohlsen (Eds.), *Family counseling and therapy* (pp. 214–244). Itasca, IL: Peacock.

Goldenberg, I., & Goldenberg, H. (1991). *Family therapy: An overview*. Pacific Grove, CA: Brooks/Cole.

Goldenberg, I., & Goldenberg, H. (2000). *Family therapy: An overview* (5th ed.). Pacific Grove, CA: Brooks/Cole.

Gurman, A. S., & Kniskern, D. P. (Eds.). (1986). *Handbook of family therapy* (2nd ed.). New York: Brunner/Mazel.

Horne, A. M. (2000). *Family counseling and therapy* (3rd ed.). Itasca, IL: Peacock.

Satir, V. (1972). *Peoplemaking*. Palo Alto, CA: Science and Behavior Books.

Satir, V. M. (1976). *Making contact*. Millbrae, CA: Celestial Arts.

Satir, V. M. (1982). The therapist and family therapy: Process model. In A. M. Horne & M. M. Ohlsen (Eds.),

Family counseling and therapy (pp. 12–42). Itasca, IL: Peacock.

Satir, V. M. (1983). *Conjoint family therapy* (3rd ed.). Palo Alto, CA: Science and Behavior Books. (Original work published 1964; 2nd ed., 1967).

Satir, V. M. (1988). *The new peoplemaking*. Palo Alto, CA: Science and Behavior Books.

Satir, V. M., & Baldwin, M. (1983). *Satir step by step*. Palo Alto, CA: Science and Behavior Books.

Satir, V. M., & Bitter, J. R. (1991). Human validation process model. In A. M. Horne & J. L. Passmore (Eds.), *Family counseling and therapy* (2nd ed., pp. 13–45). Itasca, IL: Peacock.

Satir, V. M., & Bonner, J. (1991). *The Satir model*. Palo Alto, CA: Science and Behavior Books, Inc.

Satir, V. M., Stachowiak, J., & Taschman, H. A. (1975). *Helping families to change*. New York: Aronson.

Sprenkle, D. H., Blow, A. J., & Dickey, M. H. (1999). Common factors and other nontechnique variables in marriage and family therapy. In M. Hubble, B. Duncan, & S. Miller (Eds.), *The heart and soul of change: What works in therapy* (pp. 329–359). Washington, DC: American Psychological Association.

Stanton, M. D,, & Shadish, W. R. (1997). Outcome, attrition, and family-couples treatment for drug abuse: A meta-analysis and review of the controlled, comparative studies. *Psychological Bulletin, 122,* 170–191.

Walsh, W. (1980). *A primer in family therapy.* Springfield, IL: Charles C Thomas.

Winter, J. (1989). *Family research project. Treatment outcomes and results.* Unpublished manuscript, Family Institute of Virginia, Richmond.

Woods, M. D., & Martin, D. (1984). The work of Virginia Satir: Understanding her theory and technique. *American Journal of Family Therapy, 12*(4), 3–11.

3

Bowenian Theory

MAJOR THEORIST: Murray Bowen

Key Terms:

Differentiation of self
Emotional cutoff
Emotional neutrality
Emotional system
Fusion
Genogram
Projection process
Triangles
Undifferentiated family ego mass

owenian theory, a first-generation model of family therapy, has been described as having the most comprehensive view of human behavior and human problems of any approach to family treatment (Nichols & Schwartz, 1991). The primary emphasis in this model is to provide a theory of family functioning. The model of therapy derived from this theory is a secondary concern. Relative to other models of family therapy, Bowenian theory tends to have a more intellectual orientation and less of an emotional or experiential focus.

Bowenian theory was originally formulated by Murray Bowen and was referred to by the name "family systems theory." Because that name was sometimes confused with general systems theory, it was abandoned and replaced with the name Bowenian theory. Bowenian theory is a first-generation family therapy model.

Trained as a physician, Murray Bowen elected to specialize in psychiatry. During his residency at the Menninger Clinic, Bowen became increasingly dissatisfied with psychoanalytic concepts that were not amenable to validation by conventionally accepted scientific methods. Consequently, he began to develop a new theory that Kerr and Bowen (1988) later characterized as "a natural systems theory, designed to fit precisely with the principles of evolution and the human as an evolutionary being" (p. 360). Bowen and his colleagues continued to refine Bowenian theory after Bowen's move to the National Institute for Mental Health (NIMH) in Bethesda, Maryland, in 1954. At NIMH, Bowen had entire families admitted to the psychiatric research ward. Research with these families was directed by Bowenian theory, and the theory was extended and modified when practitioners were confronted with new or incompatible information. During Bowen's 5 years at NIMH, the focus of his research was on families with schizophrenic offspring, particularly the symbiotic relationship observed between mothers and their children. Eventually, however, the theory evolved to include the entire family and to address other types of families as well. As Bowen (1978) stated:

> Since that time the effort has been to extend the theoretical orientation from a family concept of schizophrenia to a family theory of emotional illness and to adapt the family psychotherapy to the entire range of emotional illness. (p. 105)

In 1959, Bowen left NIMH to serve on the faculty of the school of medicine at Georgetown University, where he further developed his theory and, in 1968, initiated a postgraduate training program in family therapy. At the Georgetown University Family Center, work continues on Bowenian theory and its therapeutic application. Murray Bowen died in 1990. Prominent figures in Bowenian theory today include Michael Kerr, Daniel Papero, Philip Guerin, and Thomas Fogerty.

Historical Influences

The emphasis on scientific rigor is salient in Bowen's work. The natural sciences and the concept of evolution served as models for Bowen's concept of psychology as a science, and Charles Darwin and Sigmund Freud had a significant impact on Bowen's thinking. Many concepts in Bowenian theory are descended from psychoanalytic thought. Bowen himself was in analysis for 13 years.

As opposed to being based on general systems theory, which emphasizes feedback mechanisms and self-regulating systems, Bowen's model is closer to natural systems theory. Natural systems theory suggests that the family, like all systems (e.g., ant colonies, tides, or the solar system), is guided by processes common in nature (Goldenberg & Goldenberg, 2000).

Philosophy

Bowenian theory is rooted in the idea that all humans have a common evolutionary heritage at primitive levels of functioning that have an impact on behavior (e.g., reflexive and reactive emotional responses). This aspect of functioning is universal and transcends historical and cultural contexts.

Two counterbalancing life forces are relevant to family functioning (Papero, 1991): individuality, a natural force rooted in an instinctual drive to be a self-contained independent organism; and togetherness, a natural force rooted in an instinctual need for others and a sense of being connected to another person or a group. These forces are pervasive in that all relationships have a dynamic interplay of individuality and togetherness.

Humans have both emotional systems and intellectual systems. When these systems operate in a separate but harmonious manner, the individual has a choice between reacting in an emotional fashion and reacting in an intellectual fashion in any given situation. When anxiety escalates emotional intensity, the intellectual and emotional systems become fused. Consequently, thinking and behavior become more emotionally determined and choice is compromised.

The family is an emotionally interdependent unit. A change in one part of the family system will evoke changes in other parts and in the entire family. However, behaviors in a family tend to crystallize in regular patterns through time. These patterns are frequently repeated in several generations. Families exert a strong influence to promote the conformity of each member's behavior (i.e., homeostasis). The family establishes the emotional climate and behaviors that members will re-create in nonfamily settings.

In addition to being applied to the family unit, Bowenian theory also can be applied to other kinds of social groups, including those involved with work, religion, and politics. These groups manifest emotional processes similar to those of the family unit.

Theoretical Tenets

Eight major concepts constitute the core of Bowenian theory. These interrelated concepts build on the cornerstone of the theory, the emotional system, which Bowen (1975) described as follows:

> It [the emotional system] includes the force that biology defines as instinct, reproduction, the automatic activity controlled by the autonomic nervous system, subjective emotional and feeling states and the forces that govern relationship systems. . . . In broad terms, the emotional system governs the "dance of life" in all living things. (p. 380)

Another key term in early Bowenian work is "undifferentiated family ego mass." This term refers to the intense emotional oneness in a family that causes emotionality, which, in turn, interferes with thinking, and prevents the individual's differentiation from the family (Bowen, 1978). Hall noted that Bowen no longer uses this term (the term "fusion" currently is preferred), yet the eight core concepts that constitute Bowenian theory were based in part on this term (Hall, 1981). The eight core concepts of Bowenian theory are:

- *Nuclear Family Emotional Process:* This concept describes the range of relationship patterns in the family system. There are four mechanisms used by family members to manage anxiety when it becomes too intense in the nuclear family. Within a family, all four mechanisms may be employed, but the family may predominantly use one or perhaps more:

  - *Emotional Distance:* In a fused family system with high levels of anxiety, a family member may increase interpersonal distance when he or she is unable to manage emotional reactivity (Bowen, 1978). Frequently this can result in more distance than the individual actually desires.
  - *Marital Conflict:* The amount of conflict in a marriage typically is a function of the degree of fusion in the relationship and the intensity of the underlying anxiety (Papero, 1991). A cyclic process may occur in which conflict is followed by emotional distance, a period of warm togetherness, then an increase in tension that precipitates another conflict and the perpetuation of the cycle.
  - *Transmission of the Problem to a Child:* Problems and anxiety between spouses can be avoided by parental focus on one or more children. The most common pattern is for the mother to focus much of her emotional energy on a child while the father supports this via reciprocal distancing. The focused-on child has increased reactivity and fusion of intellect and emotion and is most vulnerable to the development of problems.
  - *Dysfunction in a Spouse:* Reciprocal roles may develop in the couple with one member being inadequate or dysfunctional and the other being overly adequate in an effort to compensate. This pattern can increase and solidify to the extent that the low-functioning individual develops a chronic mental or physical malady.

■ *Differentiation of Self:* In the context of an emotional system, this concept refers to the relative degree of autonomy an individual maintains while remaining in meaningful relationships with others. Highly differentiated individuals have a more fully integrated, solid self (i.e., a concept of self that is nonnegotiable with others), and their behavior is guided primarily by their intellect. Individuals with low levels of differentiation are guided predominantly by their pseudo-self (i.e., a concept of self that is negotiable with others), and their behavior tends to be directed by their emotions. Signs of higher levels of differentiation include:

  □ Clear sense of self in proximity to partner
  □ Self-regulation of own fears and anxieties
  □ Nonreactivity to partner's anxieties
  □ Toleration of discomfort for growth

■ *Triangles:* A triangle is the basic unit of interdependence in the family emotional system. When anxiety in a dyad reaches an uncomfortable level, a third person is predictably drawn into the emotional field of the twosome. Triangles in a family may lay dormant and not be overtly apparent, yet these triangles can be activated during times of stress. In general, the higher the fusion in a family, the greater the efforts to triangulate to relieve tension. The least differentiated person in the system is the most vulnerable to being triangulated.

■ *Family Projection Process:* Bowenian theory posits that the parents' level of differentiation is passed on to one or more of the offspring. Typically, one child in a family will have increased emotional involvement with one of the parents. This overinvolvement can range from the parent being excessively solicitous to the parent being extremely hostile. The dynamic impairs the child's capacity to function effectively in social settings. The degree of differentiation of the parents and the level of stress in the family determine the intensity of the family projection process.

■ *Emotional Cutoff:* In an attempt to deal with the fusion and lack of differentiation in their intimate relationships, family members or segments of the extended system may distance themselves from one another and become emotionally divorced (Hall, 1981). Although the cut-off individual may appear to handle the relationship with the family, the individual remains more vulnerable to other intense relationships. Kerr (1981) suggested that emotional cutoff indicates a problem (fusion between generations), solves a problem (decreases anxiety associated with family contact), and creates a problem (isolates individuals who could benefit from contact). As a result of the cutoff, the individual remains stuck in the emotional system of the family and may be less able to respond effectively to problem-solving situations. The consequent dysfunction can also manifest itself in other ways, such as superficial relationships, physical illness, depression, and impulsive behaviors (Walsh, 1980).

- *Multigenerational Transmission Process:* The strong tendency to repeat impairing patterns of emotional behavior in successive generations culminates in lowered levels of differentiation of self for certain members of the younger generations (Hall, 1981). Bowen proposeed that individuals at equivalent levels of differentiation find each other and marry and may have one or more children at even lower levels of differentiation. This repetitive pattern results in successively lower levels of differentiation in subsequent generations. The process culminates in an ultimate level of impairment that is consistent with a diagnosis of schizophrenia.

- *Sibling Position:* Seniority and gender distribution among siblings have a strong influence on behavior (Hall, 1981). Research by Walter Toman (1969) described different roles individuals take as a result of their position in their families of origin (e.g., oldest child, younger sister, youngest child). Bowen (1978) suggested that interactive patterns between marital couples could be related to the individuals' respective roles from their families of origin. For example, two oldest children marrying could lead to competition to see who is in charge.

- *Emotional Process in Society (societal regression):* The processes that are characteristic of families also can be observed in interactions on a societal level. For example, with high anxiety and stress due to crime, unemployment, and pollution, there is a societal tendency toward emotional reactivity and a decreased likelihood for individuation through the effective use of intellectual processes. Bowen noted that the recent history of U.S. society seems to reflect this type of regression.

Perspectives on Family Function and Dysfunction

In Bowenian theory, a functional family is characterized by the viability or survival value of its emotional processes rather than by its form or structure. The viability of the family also is correlated with the family's management of tension between individuality and togetherness forces. Families in which emotional processes are flexible allow for differentiation of self of the individual family members. This type of family is characterized by open communication, a low frequency of symptomatic behaviors, and a lack of emotional cutoff. Emotional processes that are conducive to the successful adaptation of the family unit are termed "strengths" (Hall, 1981).

Dysfunction, in Bowenian theory, is termed "weakness" and denotes a low degree of viability of emotional processes. Weaknesses are destructive to the family, eventually leading to its extinction (Hall, 1981). Dysfunctional processes in a family may be manifested by high levels of emotional intensity, rigid and restrictive relationships (e.g., dependency or isolation), low levels of individual differentiation of self, and overt symptoms in individual family members.

As previously mentioned, Bowen postulated that individuals with similar levels of differentiation tend to seek each other out and marry. Individuals with low levels of differentiation who marry are more likely to have more intense levels of fusion, which leads to the previously described problems. Through the multigenerational process, dysfunction in one generation is passed on to members of the next generation and tends to be perpetuated in this manner.

Assessment and Diagnosis

Therapists following Bowenian theory avoid pathologizing one family member (frequently termed the "identified patient"). Instead, they conceptualize the problem in terms of the entire family system. Assessment begins as information about family processes is collected in the initial sessions. Bowenian therapists may structure the family evaluation in a variety of ways. Kerr (1981, p. 252) offered the following general framework for an evaluation interview:

- History of the presenting problem
- History of the nuclear family
- History of the husband's extended family system
- History of the wife's extended family system
- Conclusion

Information that is gathered can be documented on a family genogram, providing a visual depiction of family processes. The genogram, an example of which is presented in Figure 3.1, is readily identified as a key tool in Bowenian theory. Frequently, nodal events (i.e., events subsequent to which family functioning has shifted) such as births, divorces, and deaths are documented on a family genogram. Characteristics of the family system, such as triangles and emotional cutoffs, can be represented so that the multigenerational processes that have shaped the nuclear family can be illuminated. A good source to guide the construction of a genogram is McGoldrick and Gerson (1985).

The family genogram that is constructed serves as a blueprint that enables the therapist to understand the emotional system. It also functions as a guide to treatment and may be shared with the family as a component of the therapeutic process.

Goals of Treatment

The most important goal of the Bowenian treatment process is to improve differentiation of the self (Bowen, 1978). With increased differentiation, individual family members are better able to tolerate

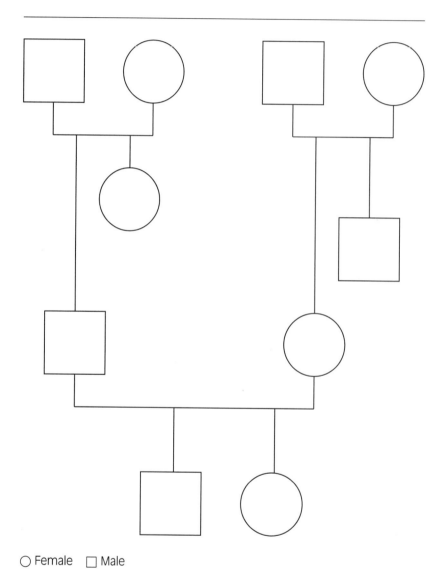

○ Female   □ Male

FIGURE 3.1

Basic Family Genogram

anxiety and access their intellectual functions. Decreased emotional reactivity and enhanced intellectual functioning are achieved through the attainment of other goals of treatment in this model. As noted by Bowen (1978):

> A goal in family therapy is to reduce the level of anxiety, to improve the level of responsible open communication within the family, and to reduce the irresponsible, underground communication of secrets and gossip to others. (p. 291)

Another goal of treatment is to decrease emotional cutoff and work to resolve unfinished business with the family of origin.

In the Bowenian model, therapists establish treatment goals for themselves that are crucial to the family's attainment of their goals (Kerr & Bowen, 1988). These goals include:

- reducing anxiety in the emotional field to improve the functional level of differentiation of self and reduce symptoms

- improving the basic level of differentiation to increase the adaptability of the person to intense emotional fields

Symptom reduction and decreased anxiety can occur relatively quickly in treatment (i.e., from several sessions to several months of treatment); improvement in the basic level of differentiation is a long-term process that can take a number of years.

Treatment Process

A primary concern in the treatment process was stated by Bowen (1978) as follows:

> Progress in therapy depends on the therapist's ability to relate meaningfully to the family without becoming emotionally entangled in the family system. (p. 312)

The therapeutic process includes six major steps:

1. Exploring the presenting problem

2. Working with the family to develop the family genogram
3. Using systemic questions to gain information about family relationships
4. Broadening the focus to larger family systems
5. Giving feedback to clients
6. Using techniques to facilitate changes

Kerr and Bowen (1988) suggested using the following questions in the process:

■ Who initiated the therapy?

■ What is the symptom, and which family member or family relationship is symptomatic?

■ What is the immediate relationship system (this usually means the nuclear family) of the symptomatic person?

■ What are the patterns of emotional functioning in the nuclear family?

■ What is the intensity of the emotional process in the nuclear family?

■ What influences that intensity—an overload of stressful events or a low level of adaptiveness?

■ What is the nature of the extended family systems, particularly in terms of their stability and availability?

■ What is the degree of emotional cutoff from each extended family system?

■ What is the prognosis?

■ What are important directions for therapy?

If the therapist remains de-triangulated and the family is able to interact in an atmosphere of low anxiety and reactivity, progress will occur. Bowen (1978) described the successful treatment process as follows:

> After the family anxiety subsides and the spouses are more capable of reflection, individuality forces begin to surface in one spouse. This occurs as the spouse begins to focus more on the part

> the self plays in the relationship problems, to decrease blaming of
> the other for one's own discomfort and unhappiness, and to accept
> responsibility for changing self. (p. 315)

The therapist may work with a marital couple, the entire family, or just one individual from the family. The configuration of individuals seen by the therapist may change as treatment progresses.

Techniques

Bowenian theory is not technique oriented relative to other models of family therapy. The following list represents the most common techniques used in this model. All of the techniques are focused on reducing anxiety and reactivity in the family.

- *Genograms:* The most critical and compulsory technique in the model, genograms are visual representations of at least three generations of the multigenerational family. Genograms organize information about a family in a standardized manner and provide a way to visualize family dynamics (e.g., triangles, cutoffs, pathology). A master genogram can capture the family history to the present. Multiple working genograms can represent specific problem situations and can track progress in therapy.

- *Emotional Neutrality:* The therapist can best facilitate change by remaining objective in sessions and staying de-triangulated from the system. By staying outside the emotionality of the family, the therapist can better resist the reactivity of triangulation.

- *Factual Questioning:* By asking frequent factual questions, the therapist can keep the family focused on specific dynamics rather than an emotionality and reactivity. Family members may be asked to answer or speak to the therapist instead of each other.

- *Didactic Teaching:* By teaching the family about emotional systems (tenets of the model), the therapist can help family members think more objectively about the problem situation and their role in the multigenerational system. This didactic teaching provides a cognitive framework to which the family can refer in understanding problems.

- *Role Playing:* This technique offers clients an active way to understand and change specific dynamics or relationships in the family. Role playing may be particularly useful in dealing with fusion in the system.

- *Empty Chair:* This psychodramatic technique is a form of role playing in which an individual speaks to an absent family member to understand or resolve past or present difficulties. The empty chair technique is particularly useful for resolving cutoffs.

- *Journaling:* With this technique, the client keeps written accounts of feelings and expressions during times of struggle and peace. The journal entries can be shared with the therapist and family during sessions to bring about discussion regarding family relationships and conflicts.

- *Letter Writing:* With this technique, family members write letters to one another or letters addressing feelings about familial situations. This technique can be particularly powerful when a member writes a letter regarding feelings of grief or loss about a relationship or regarding part of him- or herself that has been altered by injury, accident, or loss of a close relationship. The letters may be mailed or remain private.

- *Multiple Family Therapy:* In Bowen's use of this technique, families meet together as a group, and the therapist works with one family at a time while the other families observe. The process is employed to enhance the learning of a family through observation of the emotional processes of other families in therapy.

Role of the Therapist

The primary task of the therapist is to remain detached from the family emotional process. The therapist closely observes the process of communication, gains an understanding of the family dynamics, and creates in the session an atmosphere in which work toward differentiation can occur. By maintaining the "I-Position" (i.e., holding to one's position based on thinking rather than emotion despite emotional pressures from the family), the therapist enables the family to touch on important issues and elicits calm, thoughtful responses (Bowen, 1978).

Bowen pioneered the practice of family therapists' addressing their own issues by increasing their differentiation from their families of origin. This personal work by the therapist fosters decreased reactivity when dealing with families and an increased ability to remain detached.

Evaluation of the Bowenian Model

Bowenian theory provides a good example of a working theory because research continues to expand both the theory and its application. Currently, various staff members at the Georgetown University Family Center are using this model to guide their work with clients with AIDS, cancer, and other challenging human concerns (Papero, 1991). Extrapolation of Bowenian theory to societal processes is another current area of study, as is work linking family systems with other sciences.

Evidence of the clinical efficacy of Bowenian theory has been based primarily on clinical observation and experience because of Bowen's focus on integrating theory and practice and because of the difficulty associated with experimental testing of the theory (Nichols, 1984). When judged on the criteria for a good theory (Combs, 1989), this model fares relatively well. Bowen's theory is viewed as comprehensive, consistent, useful, and elegant (Nichols, 1984). As previously noted, a shortcoming is the paucity of controlled experimentation to validate the theoretical tenets of the model and to assess its clinical efficacy.

Bowen is seen as one of the pioneers in the development of family theory and therapy (Broderick & Schrader, 1981). Bowenian theory has had a significant impact on the field of family therapy by bringing attention to the relevance of the wider kinship network of family functioning. It has also influenced other models of family therapy, particularly the development of network therapy by Speck and Attneave (Nichols, 1984).

References

Bowen, M. (1975). Family therapy after twenty years. In D. Freedman & K. Dyrud (Eds.), *American handbook of psychiatry,* Vol. 5 (pp. 367–392). New York: Basic Books.

Bowen, M. (1978). *Family therapy in clinical practice.* New York: Jason Aronson.

Broderick, C. B., & Schrader, S. S. (1981). The history of professional marriage and family therapy. In A. S. Gurman & D. P. Kniskern (Eds.), *Handbook of family therapy* (pp. 5–35). New York: Brunner/Mazel.

Combs, A. W. (1989). A *theory of therapy.* Needham Heights, MA: Allyn & Bacon.

Goldenberg, I., & Goldenberg, H. (2000). *Family therapy: An overview* (5th ed.). Pacific Grove, CA: Brooks/Cole.

Hall, C. M. (1981). *The Bowen family theory and its uses.* New York: Jason Aronson.

Kerr, M. E. (1981). Family systems theory and therapy. In A. A. Gurman & D. P. Kniskern (Eds.), *Handbook of family therapy* (pp. 226–264). New York: Brunner/Mazel.

Kerr, M. E., & Bowen, M. (1988). *Family evaluation: An approach based on Bowen theory.* New York: Norton.

McGoldrick, M., & Gerson, R. (1985). *Genograms in family assessment.* New York: Norton.

Nichols, M. P. (1984). *Family therapy: Concepts and methods.* New York: Gardner Press.

Nichols, M. P., & Schwartz, R. C. (1991). *Family therapy: Concepts and methods* (2nd ed.). Boston: Allyn & Bacon.

Papero, D. V. (1991). The Bowen theory. In A. M. Horne & J. L. Passmore (Eds.), *Family counseling and therapy* (pp. 47–75). Itasca, IL: F. E. Peacock.

Toman, W. (1969). *Family constellation.* New York: Springer.

Walsh, W. (1980). *A primer of family therapy.* Springfield, IL: Charles C. Thomas.

4

Structural Family Therapy

MAJOR THEORIST: Salvador Minuchin

Key Terms:

Boundaries
Enactment
Family mapping
Family structure
Joining/Accommodating
Marking boundaries
Subsystems

ike communication/validation family therapy and Bowenian theory, structural family therapy is a seminal model of family therapy. It is based on the fundamental concepts underlying general structuralist thought. Structuralism approaches all human phenomena with the intent of identifying the codes that regulate human relationships. No other common name is used for this theory.

Structural family therapy is primarily credited to Salvador Minuchin, a psychiatrist born and raised in Argentina. Minuchin's early life experiences include being raised in a huge extended family of over 200 cousins and many family friends (Minuchin, 1974). This left him with a lasting impression of the social context within which human beings function. Professional experiences that shaped Minuchin's thinking include work with families in Israel, development of a therapy approach for low income/minority families through the Wiltwych School for Boys in New York, family therapy with psychosomatic patients, and involvement with the Philadelphia Child Guidance Clinic (Aponte & Van Deusen, 1981). Minuchin continues to practice family therapy, supervise, and teach. He is the author of numerous articles and books on family therapy.

Historical Influences

The influence of Alfred Adler, particularly his focus on the social, goal-oriented aspect of humans, is apparent in structural family therapy. Adler's concepts of family constellation, the positive nature of humans, and the ability of humans to change served as a foundation for Minuchin's basic theoretical formulations. Ortega y Gasset's emphasis on the interaction of individuals with their environment is reflected in Minuchin's focus on the contextual and environmental influences affecting behavior. In addition, systemic thinking, as developed by anthropologist Gregory Bateson, is a fundamental aspect of structural family therapy.

Minuchin worked with families in a variety of settings and cultures. His diverse experience with these families and his frustration with traditional psychoanalytic therapy served as a catalyst for his development of a more pragmatic, directive, and problem-oriented form of family intervention. Braulio Montalvo, a psychiatrist with whom Minuchin collaborated at Wiltwych, greatly influenced Minuchin's theory and clinical style (Minuchin, 1974). Minuchin's association with other individuals in the field of family therapy, such as Harry Aponte, Jay Haley, and other colleagues at the Philadelphia Child Guidance Clinic, helped to further refine the theory and practice of structural family therapy.

Philosophy

The philosophy behind structural family therapy focuses attention on the present and future. According to this theory the history of the family is manifest in the present, and therefore it is accessible through interventions in the here and now. Further, humans are social creatures and must be viewed holistically within the context of their social systems. Environmental factors are given priority over hereditary factors.

The reciprocal nature of systemic causality (e.g., an individual's behavior influences and is influenced by his or her social system) is acknowledged. In addition, process is emphasized over content (e.g., the "how" of communication is more important than the "what").

Structural family therapy also holds that the family is a microcosm of the social milieu and that functional and dysfunctional behaviors are taught and perpetuated by the family. The whole (family) and the parts (family members) can properly be explained only in terms of the relations that exist between the parts (Lane, 1970).

Theoretical Tenets

■ *Family Structure:* According to the structural family therapy model, an invisible web of complementary demands and expectations regulates the family. These family transactions, which make up the family structure, determine how members relate and can be verbal or nonverbal, known or unknown. A family's uniqueness is determined by the idiosyncratic repetitive transactions that make up the family's patterns of functioning. These transactions regulate behavior in two ways: A power hierarchy exists that dictates the authority and decision making in the family, and mutual expectations formed by negotiations over time are determined and fulfilled by individuals in the family.

■ *Subsystems:* The components of the family's structure that exist to carry out various family tasks are called subsystems. Subsystems can be formed on the basis of generation, interests, or specific family functions. Family members may belong to several subsystems at the same time. The most prominent and important subsystems in the family are the following:

□ *Adult Subsystem:* Sometimes termed the spousal or marital subsystem, this component of a family system typically includes the spousal dyad, or adult significant others, and teaches the children about intimacy and commitment.

□ *Parental Subsystem:* This subsystem is usually composed of the parents but may include members of the extended family (e.g., grandmother). The parental subsystem has the major responsibility for proper child rearing, guidance, limit setting, and discipline.

□ *Sibling Subsystem:* Generally including the children in a family, this subsystem serves as a child's first peer group. In the sibling subsystem, children learn negotiation, cooperation, competition, mutual support, and attachment to friends.

■ *Boundaries:* Subsystem boundaries are determined by sets of rules that define who participates in the subsystem and how the individuals participate. The nature of the boundaries has an impact on the functioning of the subsystem as well as on the entire family unit. Minuchin described three types of boundaries that lie on a continuum from very rigid to very diffuse:

□ *Rigid Boundaries:* A subsystem with rigid boundaries permits minimal interaction or communication with other subsystems. Individuals may be isolated and forced to function autonomously. Rigid boundaries provide maximum privacy. The subsystem may become disengaged from the rest of the family.

□ *Clear Boundaries:* Clear boundaries promote open communication and privacy such that subsystems can operate freely to fulfill their functions in the family system. These boundaries are essentially a midpoint between the extremes of rigid and diffuse.

□ *Diffuse Boundaries:* Subsystems with diffuse boundaries are characterized by poorly defined membership and functions. Task completion is rarely accomplished. Diffuse boundaries provide minimal privacy and maximum interaction. Lines of authority and responsibility are not clearly drawn, and family members may be overinvolved with one another.

■ *Adaptation to Stress:* This concept refers to how families adapt to tense situations caused by internal and external sources of stress impinging on the family system. According to the structural family therapy model, every family attempts to adapt to stress in ways that will preserve the integrity of the structure and thereby maintain homeostasis (Colapinto, 1991). If a family displays rigid responses to stress, unhealthy patterns will occur in the system and already existing problems will be exacerbated. Minuchin identified four sources of stress that affect families directly:

□ Stressful contact of one member with extrafamilial forces (e.g., a parent's work difficulties that are brought home and affect other family members)

□ Stressful contact of the whole family with extrafamilial forces (e.g., an economic recession affects the family's financial resources)

□ Stress occurring at developmental or transitional points in the family (e.g., children leaving home for school, for work, or to establish their own independence)

□ Stress related to idiosyncratic problems (e.g., the presence of a chronically ill family member)

■ *Developmental Family Life Stages:* The structural family therapy model posits that the family evolves in stages of increasing complexity. The family's pervasive task throughout this process is to blend the diversity of individual growth with the unity of membership in the family system. Minuchin described four stages of development that occur in many families:

☐ *Couple Formation:* The marital dyad forms a functional system by negotiating boundaries (e.g., in-law interactions), reconciling divergent lifestyles, and developing rules regarding conflict and cooperation.

☐ *Young Children:* The spousal subsystem reorganizes to adapt to the functions requisite of parenthood.

☐ *School Age and Adolescent Children:* The family interacts with the school system, and intrafamily structures are modified to make this adjustment (e.g., homework, extracurricular activities). As the children grow into adolescence, the family deals with issues around peer influences, loss of parental control, and the initial stages of the child's eventual emancipation.

☐ *Grown Children:* Parents and grown children who have emancipated modify parent-child interactions to adult-adult interactions.

The family is seen as a living, open system interacting with the environment (Colapinto, 1991). The rules of the family provide structure by which operations can occur that meet the needs of the family members and the family as a whole. Substructures within the family system interact according to rules that serve as boundaries between subsystems. Internal and external stressors necessitate adaptation of the family structure to maintain homeostasis. One predictable type of stressor is the developmental process experienced by most family systems.

Perspectives on Family Function and Dysfunction

From a structural perspective, functional and dysfunctional levels are determined by the adequacy of the fit of a family's structural organization to the requirements of operation within the environmental context. A functional family is characterized by transactions that serve to meet the needs of the individuals in the family and the family unit as a whole. Typically, functional families are characterized by structures that are adaptable and well defined.

A dysfunctional family system occurs when a stressor overloads the family's adaptive and coping mechanisms such that family members' needs are not adequately met. Frequently, the stressor is due to the changing conditions associated with the family development process. Rather than modify the family structure to adapt to the stressor, the family increases the rigidity of the preexisting inadequate structure. The family system's rigidity and inability to complete the necessary developmental task can result in dysfunction. Usually, one family member (the "identified patient") will manifest the symptom for the family and therein serve as the safety valve for the family by expressing system dysfunction (Friesen, 1985).

The structural family model classifies pathology into four general forms, noting that a family may exhibit several overlapping types of pathology. The four general forms of pathology are as follows:

- *Pathology of Boundaries:* Subsystem boundaries that are too permeable (enmeshed system) or too rigid (disengaged system) interfere with the adaptive transmission of information between subsystems.

- *Pathology of Alliances:* Intrafamilial relationships that are not conducive to healthy functioning are formed on the basis of a common interest. The two primary types of alliance pathology are (a) conflict detouring or scapegoating (e.g., a family reduces tension by blaming problems on one family member) and (b) inappropriate cross-generational coalitions (e.g., members of different generations of a family join together against a third member of the family).

- *Pathology of Triads:* Inherently unstable family arrangements are formed in which two members side against a third member. These arrangements are also termed "coalitions" (e.g., mother and son against father).

- *Pathology of Hierarchy:* Here, the functional decision-making hierarchy in which the parents are in charge is subverted by an alternative arrangement (e.g., father and child form the parental subunit excluding mother).

Assessment and Diagnosis

The therapist develops working hypotheses regarding family structure based on observations of family interactions. Problems are defined in ways that make the problems amenable to change. Interventions designed to effect structural change and therein achieve therapy goals are derived from the working hypotheses.

Diagnosis is achieved through the structural process of *joining*. Minuchin called this type of diagnosis an interactional or "structural diagnosis" (Minuchin, 1974). A structural diagnosis is an ongoing, constantly evolving process in structural family therapy that is based on data from six major areas:

1. The family structure, including its preferred transactional patterns and the alternative patterns available.

2. The system's flexibility and its capacity for elaboration and restructuring (e.g., shifting coalitions and subsystems in response to changing circumstances).

3. The family system's resonance, reflecting its sensitivity to individual members' input. High sensitivity reflects an enmeshed system; low sensitivity reflects a disengaged system.

4. The family life context, including the sources of stress and support in the family's ecology.

5. The family's developmental stage and its performance of the tasks appropriate to that stage.

6. The identified patient's symptoms and the manner in which they are used to maintain the family's preferred transactional patterns.

The information gathered from the structural diagnosis process can be expressed visually in the form of a therapeutic map (see Figure 4.1). The map facilitates the generation of working hypotheses, identifies restructuring techniques that may be effective, and establishes short-term and long-term treatment goals. The map also serves as an ongoing evaluation of the therapeutic process and may be shared with the family at appropriate intervals.

Basic map for two-parent family, two children, clear boundaries

H	W	ADULT
F	M	PARENTAL
B	G	SIBLING

Basic map for single parent with diffuse boundaries between subsystems

	W	ADULT
	M	PARENTAL
B	G	SIBLING

Blended family with two children living with the biological mother and the stepfather and visiting with the biological father and stepmother, with rigid boundaries and parental conflict

H	W		H	W	
SF	M		F	SM	PARENTAL
B	G		B	G	SIBLING

(ADULT / PARENTAL / SIBLING)

SYMBOLS

Clear boundary _ _ _ _ _ _ _ _ _ _
Rigid boundary _____
Diffuse boundary ....

Mother	M
Father	F
Stepmother	SM
Stepfather	SF

Husband	H
Wife	W
Boy	B
Girl	G
Therapist	Th
Coalition	}
Conflict	___] [___
Affiliation	=
Detouring	———→

FIGURE 4.1

Structural Family Therapy Therapeutic Maps

Goals of Treatment

The overriding goals of structural family therapy are to solve problems in the family and to change the underlying systemic structure. These goals are achieved through the attainment of smaller goals specific to the identified needs as determined by the structural diagnosis and to the particular stage in the therapeutic process (e.g., successful joining with the family in the early stages in therapy); the process of joining is described in the next section.

Treatment Process

Minuchin saw treatment as structural change that modifies the family's functioning so the family can better perform necessary tasks. Once the therapist has initiated change, the processes will be maintained by the family's self-regulating mechanisms. Because the family is a dynamic system in continual movement, the steps in the therapeutic process may overlap and recycle in "kaleidoscopic sequence" (Minuchin, 1974). Given this caveat, the typical steps in the treatment process of structural family therapy are as follows:

1. *Joining /Accommodating:* The therapist adjusts to the communication style and perceptions of family members to "join" with the system (Minuchin, 1974). The goal in this stage is to establish an effective therapeutic relationship with the family. Three techniques that are particularly useful in facilitating this process include tracking, maintenance, and mimesis.
2. *Structural Diagnosis:* The therapist carries out a continuous process of observation, hypothesis testing, and reformulation relevant to the family's structure and transactions. A goal in this stage is to develop a framework of information relevant to the problem in the family system that is amenable to structural intervention. Mapping is common in this stage.
3. *Restructuring:* The therapist utilizes therapeutic interventions that bring about change through modification in the family structure. The goal in this stage (and an indicator for termination readiness) is development of a family structure capable of dealing with future stressful situations in appropriate ways.

Techniques

Techniques in structural family therapy are employed to achieve the goals of the therapeutic process. These techniques can be categorized as joining/accommodating techniques or restructuring techniques. The following list of techniques is not exhaustive, and Friesen (1985) noted that various techniques from strategic family therapy are often utilized by structural family therapists as well.

- *Joining or Accommodating Techniques:* The primary goal of joining or accommodating techniques is to establish an effective therapeutic relationship. Minuchin considered that these techniques also serve a concomitant restructuring function (Walsh, 1980). The three major joining/accommodating techniques are maintenance, tracking, and mimesis.
  - □ *Maintenance:* The therapist supports specific behaviors or verbalizations to increase the strength and independence of individuals, subsystems, or alliances.
  - □ *Tracking:* The therapist uses clarification, amplification, and approval of family communication to reinforce individuals and subsystems.
  - □ *Mimesis:* The therapist adopts the family's communication style and conforms to its affective range (e.g., if the family frequently uses expletives, the therapist adopts this mode of speaking).

- *Restructuring Techniques:* These techniques challenge and unbalance the family system, creating movement that forces the family to seek alternative transactions and solutions. The following are common restructuring techniques.
  - □ *Enactment:* The therapist has family members perform an interaction that may be relatively innocuous (e.g., planning an outing) or may directly relate to the presenting problems. Enactments are utilized to diagnose family structure, increase intensity, and restructure family systems.
  - □ *Reenactment:* The family is asked to re-create a situation that has already occurred. These re-creations are performed in the therapy session, and the therapist helps to explicate and create a successful outcome to a normally troublesome interactional problem.

- *Actualizing Family Transactional Patterns:* By directing the family to have a conversation or by refusing to answer a question, the therapist stimulates naturalistic family interactions so he or she can observe typical transactions.
- *Marking Boundaries:* The therapist assists the family in setting new boundary rules, renegotiating old rules, or establishing specific functions for each subsystem to strengthen diffuse boundaries or increase the permeability of rigid boundaries, thereby increasing healthy subsystem interaction.
- *Escalating Stress:* The therapist heightens tension in a family to force the family members to accept restructuring. The therapist does this by encouraging conflict when it occurs, joining alliances against other family members, and blocking dysfunctional transactional patterns that serve to decrease stress in the system.
- *Assigning Tasks:* The therapist assigns specific tasks for individuals or subsystems to accomplish in the session or at home.
- *Utilizing Symptoms:* By encouraging, de-emphasizing, or relabeling a symptom, the therapist alters the function the symptom serves in the family system (Minuchin & Fishman, 1981). This technique may also remove the secondary gain that may be inherent in the symptomology.
- *Paradoxical Injunction:* The therapist imposes a directive that places the client in a therapeutic double bind that promotes change regardless of client compliance with the directive. This technique typically is utilized when resistance to the directive is anticipated.
- *Manipulating Mood in the Family:* The therapist attempts to change the mood or pacing of the family in the session. If the family appears to be lethargic or depressed, the therapist may introduce action techniques to bring more energy into the situation. If the family is talking or moving too quickly, the therapist can use slower talking or punctuation to create a more reflective mood.
- *Support, Education, and Guidance:* The therapist provides direct instruction to teach the family to behave differently (e.g., teaching the parents to give more attention to their children).

Role of the Therapist

The therapist joins the system and uses himself or herself to transform it (Minuchin, 1981). In the role of expert, the therapist is active and directive, determining the structure of the therapy and directing the process. The therapist may use a flexible, diverse personal approach to maintain his or her freedom of movement and therapeutic leverage. The therapist's personality may be brought into the therapeutic process to further the goals of the family therapy. Minuchin (1974) provided the following eloquent description of how he has integrated his personal style with the techniques and goals of structural family therapy during client sessions:

> As a therapist, I tend to act like a distant relative. I like to tell anecdotes about my own experiences and thinking, and to include things I have read or heard that are relevant to the particular family. I try to assimilate the family's language and to build metaphors using the family's language and myths. These methods telescope time, investing an encounter between strangers with the affect of an encounter between old acquaintances. They are accommodation techniques, which are vital to the process of joining. (Minuchin, 1974, p. 122)

Evaluation of the Structural Family Therapy Model

Structural family therapy has been utilized in the treatment of family and marital problems within a variety of contexts and for families with diverse presenting concerns. Minuchin has particularly focused on psychosomatic conditions (primarily anorexia nervosa), physical abuse, divorce, blended families, and alcohol abuse. Available empirical research, such as that described in the following paragraphs, supports the efficacy of structural family therapy.

Research by Minuchin, Rosman, and Baker (1978) provides empirical support for the structural notion that psychosomatic children regulate stress between parents. This study involved examining the physiological response of anorexic children (free fatty acid level in the blood indicating stress) following their observation of parental conflict.

Outcome research for the same study suggested a 90% improvement rate when structural family therapy was utilized with families with anorexic children (Minuchin et al., 1978). These positive treatment results were maintained at follow-up evaluations of up to 2-year intervals (Nichols, 1984).

Research comparing outcome results for structural family therapy, individual therapy, and a placebo condition in the treatment of drug addicts and their families suggested better treatment outcomes for structural family therapy than for the other approaches.

The application of structural family therapy to culturally diverse groups was supported when it was found to effect positive change in Hispanic families (Szapocznik et al., 1989). However, even though structural family therapy was more effective than psychodynamic child therapy, this research did not support the basic assumption of structural family therapy regarding the mechanisms mediating symptom reduction.

Aponte and Van Deusen (1981) provided a summary of the research that has been conducted on structural family therapy. They reported that this research, despite being in the relatively early stages of development, tends to confirm many of the theoretical tenets of structural family therapy. In their overview of the outcome research based on measures of symptoms and psychosocial change in the identified patient, they described structural family therapy as effective with 73% of the cases and ineffective for the remaining 27% (Aponte & Van Deusen, 1981, p. 357). They added that relative to other studies regarding the effectiveness of family therapy as noted in Gurman and Kniskern (1981), structural family therapy appears to be at least as successful as any other current model of family therapy.

The value of this approach is further evidenced by the impact it has had on other models in the field of family therapy. A recent literature review reveals that components of structural family therapy have been combined with diverse models of therapy including behavioral, strategic, and psychodrama.

References

Aponte, H. J., & Van Deusen, J. M. (1981). Structural family therapy. In A. S. Gurman & D. P. Kniskern (Eds.), *Handbook of family therapy* (pp. 310–360). New York: Brunner/Mazel.

Colapinto, J. (1991). Structural family therapy. In A. M. Horne & J. L. Passmore (Eds.), *Family counseling and therapy* (pp. 77–106). Itasca, IL: Peacock.

Friesen, J. (1985). *Structural-strategic marriage and family therapy.* New York: Gardner Press.

Gurman, A. S., & Kniskern, D. P. (Eds.). (1981). *Handbook of family therapy.* New York: Brunner/Mazel.

Lane, M. (1970). *Introduction to structuralism.* New York: Basic Books.

Minuchin, S. (1974). *Families and family therapy.* Cambridge, MA: Harvard University Press.

Minuchin, S. (1981). Structural family therapy. In R. J. Green & J. L. Framo (Eds.), *Family therapy: Major contributions* (pp. 445–473). New York: International Universities Press.

Minuchin, S., & Fishman, C. H. (1981). *Family therapy techniques.* Cambridge, MA: Harvard University Press.

Minuchin, S., Rosman, B., & Baker, L. (1978). *Psychosomatic families: Anorexia nervosa in context.* Cambridge, MA: Harvard University Press.

Nichols, M. P. (1984). *Family therapy: Concepts and methods.* New York: Gardner Press.

Szapocznik, J., Murray, E., Scopetta, M., Hervis, O., Rio, A., Cohen, R., Rivas-Vazquez, A., & Posada, V. (1989). Structural family versus psychodynamic child therapy for problematic Hispanic boys. *Journal of Consulting and Clinical Psychology, 57,* 571–578.

Walsh, W. (1980). A *primer of family therapy.* Springfield, IL: Charles C Thomas.

5

Strategic Family Therapy

MAJOR THEORISTS: Jay Haley and Cloe Madanes

Key Terms:

Alliances
Coalitions
Directives
Hierarchy
Metaphorical tasks
Power
Prescribing the symptom
Pretend techniques

trategic family therapy is one of the major models of family therapy. Because much of it is derived from communication and structural therapies, it is considered a second-generation theory. Jay Haley described this method as therapy in which the therapist designs interventions that fit the problem. This chapter focuses on strategic family therapy as conceptualized and practiced by Jay Haley and Cloe Madanes. Readers are encouraged to review the works of other contributors to this model of family therapy as well.

Variants of strategic family therapy have branched out from the core elements developed by Haley and Madanes. Additional names used to denote this general classification of family therapy include systemic therapy, brief therapy, and problem-solving therapy. All of these variants have different emphases and nuances yet share a common origin and philosophical basis.

Jay Haley was born in 1923. His education included undergraduate work in library science at the University of California at Berkeley and graduate work in communication at Stanford. Following completion of his master's degree in 1953, Haley worked on the Project for the Study of Communication, which was directed by Gregory Bateson. Haley's involvement included research and study in the areas of hypnosis, animal behavior, schizophrenia, families, and family therapy. Haley also entered private practice in psychotherapy during this time. Along with private practice, Haley has held professorships at the University of Pennsylvania, Howard University, and the University of Maryland. He worked at the Mental Research Institute and the Philadelphia Child Guidance Clinic as well as cofounding and codirecting of the Family Therapy Institute of Washington, DC, with Cloe Madanes. A prolific writer, Haley has been the author, coauthor, or editor of numerous books and journal articles on diverse topics.

Cloe Madanes stated that her interest in psychology began when she was 14 years old. Her professional education in Argentina had a psychoanalytic orientation, and she was in analysis for 5 years. Reading an article on double-bind theory by Bateson, Jackson, Haley, and Weakland (1956) piqued Madanes's interest in families and communication. In 1965, Madanes moved to Palo Alto and began studying family therapy at the Mental Research Institute. She also worked as a research assistant for Paul Watzlawick. After 3 years, Madanes returned to Argentina, where she accepted a position as a professor and clinical supervisor of family therapy. She returned to the United States in 1971 and worked at the Philadelphia Child Guidance Clinic with Minuchin, Haley, and Montalvo. Madanes subsequently left the Child Guidance Clinic and cofounded, with Haley, the Family Therapy Institute of Washington, DC, where she presently serves as codirector.

Historical Influences

Two influences figure prominently in the origin of strategic family therapy: Bateson's work on cybernetics, systems, and communication and Erickson's use of hypnosis and paradoxical directives in therapy. The former influence derived from Haley's involvement with Bateson, Don Jackson, John Weakland, and William Fry, in Bateson's research on communication. This diverse collection of individuals composed the initial membership of the now famous Palo Alto group. Their research on the families of individuals with schizophrenia spawned the "double-bind" concept, which was reported in the article "Toward a Theory of Schizophrenia" (Bateson et al., 1956). This article engendered an interest in the family treatment of schizophrenia.

Erickson's influence on strategic family therapy was felt when Haley and Weakland began weekend tutelage under Erickson at his home in Phoenix, Arizona. This initiated a long-standing collaboration between Erickson and Haley in which Haley studied and chronicled Erickson's clinical work. Haley described Erickson's pragmatic, innovative, and sometimes incomprehensible work in his books *Strategies of Psychotherapy* (1963) and *Uncommon Therapy* (1973).

Haley's collaboration with Salvador Minuchin and Braulio Montalvo at the Philadelphia Child Guidance Clinic facilitated a sharing of ideas and the eventual convergence of strategic and structural family therapy models in numerous areas.

The strategic family therapy model continues to be refined by Arthur Bodin, Carlos Sluzki, Olga Silverstein, and Peggy Papp in their ongoing research and clinical practice.

Philosophy

Strategic family therapy is based on the idea that families are rule-governed systems and can best be understood in this context. Furthermore, the presenting problem serves a function in the family that must be recognized. Symptoms are system maintained and system maintaining. Destructive ongoing cycles of interaction prevent the family or couple from achieving its basic purposes.

Developmental stages in the family life cycle are significant considerations in strategic family therapy, because stunted development can lead to problems in later stages. With this model, the focus is on the present, and insight into the cause of the problem is less important than effecting a change in behavior or functioning.

Theoretical Tenets

- *Family Patterns:* The organization of the family is reflected in characteristic family behavioral patterns that are dependable and highly predictable.

- *Hierarchy:* Within the family system there is a vertical organization that usually is related to the degree of influence one member has over another.

- *Alliances and Coalitions:* These formations within family groups and other parts of the family system make the family a distinct entity. The alliances and coalitions can alter the conventional hierarchy of the family (e.g., mother and daughter form a coalition against the father that undermines his authority).

- *Communication:* Two levels of communication are attended to in strategic family therapy: digital communication and analogic communication.

☐ *Digital communication* is highly technical, formal, content-oriented communication in which each statement has one referent and only that referent. Like the digital communication used by computers to transmit data to a specific recipient, this type of communication is very rigid. Problems arise when only digital communication rather than multiple levels is considered in human interactions because much of the message may be lost.

☐ *Analogic communication* has many referents and is conveyed through a family's metaphors, body language, and symbolism. The therapist's understanding of analogic communication among individuals is crucial when conceptualizing and intervening through the relational context of the presenting problem.

■ *Symptoms:* The patterns family members use to gain control of relationships within the family are called symptoms. These symptoms may become problematic within the system and are the root of the concern that brings the family into therapy.

■ *Presenting Problem:* The presenting problem is concern or issue identified by the family that resulted in involvement in treatment.

■ *Power:* The concept of power within the family structure refers to the struggle to make rules in a family. In some instances, family members fight vigorously to hold on to current family rules and interactional structures rather than changing them.

■ *Family Life Cycle:* The family life cycle is the process of development of the family that includes such stages as marriage, birth of first child, reduction in family size (e.g., children leaving home), and advanced aging. The family life cycle is an important focus in strategic family therapy because it is considered a source of familial stress. The transition between stages becomes the identified focal point of treatment. The appearance of presenting problems frequently corresponds to the family encountering a developmental process task.

Perspectives on Family Function and Dysfunction

From a strategic family therapy perspective, functional families have the characteristics of an open system. These characteristics include clear boundaries that allow adequate and predictable exchange of information within and without the family, adaptability, and organization. Haley noted that in functional families in most societies parents are at the top of the family hierarchy maintaining the authority within the family. In addition, functional families utilize effective communication processes that allow them to deal with the challenges posed by family developmental tasks and miscellaneous problems.

Three general types of problems are common in dysfunctional families (Haley, 1987). First, problem solution is often at the wrong hierarchical level. Second, these families typically deny the presence of a problem or create a problem where none exists. And third, dysfunctional families are characterized by unclear or inappropriate hierarchical structure. Haley (1976) noted that "if there is a fundamental rule of social organization, it is that an organization is in trouble when coalitions occur across levels of a hierarchy" (p. 104). When such an interactional pattern becomes crystallized in a family, symptomatic behavior in one or more family members is highly likely.

In Madanes's work, the symptom is seen as representative of the underlying relational dynamic. An example of symptom as metaphor is an asthmatic child whose presenting concerns symbolize his or her mother's feeling of being "suffocated" in her relationship with her husband. Haley (1973) noted that presenting problems frequently arise when the family encounters a developmental task in its life cycle. Symptoms are likely to occur at points of transition between stages. Some families develop problems because they fail to make the necessary transition from one stage to the next. The failure occurs when the family has difficulty mastering the tasks inherent in a stage of the life cycle. In short, the problem is not the identified patient but the way the family reacts to the stage it is approaching or has entered and attempts to adapt to it.

Assessment and Diagnosis

Assessment in strategic family therapy involves an ongoing process of observation of the relational dynamics of the family. Particularly, therapeutic attention is focused on family patterns, coalitions, alliances, communication (e.g., analogic, digital), and power. Diagnoses are framed as interactional sequences among family members that pose problems and prevent successful adaptation. Diagnostic labels that suggest pathology in a family member are avoided.

Assessment begins with the first contact with the family as the therapist begins to form initial hypotheses about family dynamics. These hypotheses are tested through ongoing observation of the family, and revisions to the hypotheses are made as needed. Frequently, diagnosis is initiated by making an intervention and then observing how the family system responds. The focus is on specific problems and the therapeutic strategies that can interrupt the patterns maintaining the problem.

Goals of Treatment

A hallmark of strategic family therapy is its primary goal of addressing the presenting problem as identified by the family. This goal was cogently stated by Haley (1987):

> The first obligation of a therapist is to change the presenting problem offered. If that is not accomplished, the therapy is a failure. Therapists should not let themselves be distracted into other matters so that they forget this primary goal. Moreover, by focusing on the symptoms the therapist gains the most leverage and has the most opportunity for bringing about change. (p. 135)

The Mental Research Institute (MRI) style of strategic family therapy has a goal of changing only the presenting problem. Haley set the more inclusive aim of also striving to alter the relational dynamics associated with the behavior. It is not a goal of strategic family therapy to work toward family insight regarding interactional processes.

Treatment Process

The treatment process in strategic family therapy is pragmatic, brief, and orchestrated by the therapist. The objective of the treatment process is to interrupt behavioral sequences to promote goal attainment. Change occurs when the therapist actively intervenes to alter the family's typical interactional patterns. As noted by Haley (1987),

> When dealing with a governed, homeostatic system that is maintained by repeating sequences of behavior, the therapist changes those sequences by shifting the ways people respond to each other because of the ways they must respond to the therapist. (p. 186)

Five basic stages can be used to describe the treatment process:

1. *Establishing a Therapeutic Relationship:* Establishing a trusting relationship with the family is a crucial component of promoting change. The therapist joins the family system by greeting and interacting with each family member. Typically the parents are engaged first, then they are asked to introduce their children. This interaction serves the purpose of allowing the therapist to observe the hierarchical structure within the family. The therapist begins to form tentative hypotheses about the family dynamics based on observations of the family (e.g., who sits by whom, who interrupts and when).

2. *Clarifying the Presenting Problem:* The objective in this stage is to form a clear understanding of which family members are involved in maintaining the problem and how this occurs. The therapist asks each family member to describe the problem. The strategy the therapist chooses regarding how and when to procure this information is very important and may differ given the particulars of the family. For example, by addressing the least involved child first, the therapist demonstrates the importance of each member of the family (Haley, 1987). The therapist must specify the problem clearly and specifically (i.e., in observable and measurable terms) so the family will know when they have successfully addressed the problem.

3. *Observing and Assessing Family Interactions:* Interactions among family members are observed by the therapist as a means of assessing system functioning. The therapist may encourage a child to engage in the problematic behavior in the session to observe the family dynamics with regard to areas of dysfunction, such as diffuse boundaries, coalitions, and triangles.

4. *Setting Goals:* The therapist assists the family in describing what life will be like at the end of treatment. A slightly different perspective or summary of the family's goal may be presented by the therapist to begin to reframe the presenting problem. Ultimately, the specific goals may be formalized through the use of a verbal or written contract.

5. *Developing a Plan:* A plan is formulated that takes into account the dysfunctional family hierarchy and the family's stage in the life cycle. The therapist has the final determination as to how to achieve the goals. The therapist may employ intervention as a therapeutic tool, using directives to create new behaviors. These directives may be rehearsed in the session but need to be carried out in real life. Interventions may not lead directly to the family goal; rather, intermediate steps may be involved as described by Hoffman (1981):

> Haley thinks of therapy in terms of a step-by-step change in the way the family is organized, so that it goes from one type of abnormal organization to another type before a more normal organization is finally achieved. By then, presumably, the symptom is no longer necessary. (p. 280)

Generally, the therapeutic process involves meeting with the entire family for weekly sessions. The duration in therapy is brief, customarily lasting 6 to 10 sessions. Toward the end of treatment, the time between sessions may be extended (e.g., 1 to 2 sessions per month). A posttreatment follow-up session may be a component of the treatment process.

Techniques

■ *Directives:* The use of directives to initiate or maintain change is the cornerstone of strategic family therapy. Directives serve three basic functions in therapy: promoting behavior change and new subjective experiences for family members, intensifying the therapist-client relationship through the use of tasks, and gathering useful information about the family by noting the family's response to the directives. Directives fall into two categories: straightforward directives and paradoxical directives. The therapist chooses and modifies directives to fit each unique situation.

☐ *Straightforward directives* are tasks designed to change the interactional sequence in the family. They can include advice, explanations, or suggestions. Straightforward directives are presented with the expectation that the family will not resist the task. Madanes (1981) stated that straightforward directives are planned with the goal of changing sequences of interaction in the family. The interventions may be employed to involve disengaged family members, promote agreement and good feeling, increase positive interchanges, provide information, and help a family organize in more functional ways. The intervention process may involve setting rules, defining generational boundaries, and establishing individual goals and plans for achieving those goals. Haley (1976) provided many suggestions for increasing the family's cooperation with the directives that are presented. Among his suggestions were for the therapist to be precise, get everyone in the family to do something, start with small tasks in the session that the family can continue at home, anticipate what may go wrong, and structure a task that fits with the performance level of the family.

☐ *Paradoxical directives* involve tasks in which success is based on the family defying the instructions or following them to an extreme point and ultimately recoiling, producing change. Typically the therapist presents these directives when he or she has reason to believe the family will resist a straightforward directive. Haley described eight steps for presenting a paradoxical directive: (1) Establish a trusting relationship with the family where change is anticipated; (2) define the problem in clear, observable terms; (3) set specific, behavioral goals; (4) design a plan that is delivered in a precise and authoritative manner; (5) disqualify the current authority on the problem; (6) deliver the paradoxical directive in a sincere manner; (7) encourage symptomatic behavior; (8) avoid taking credit for family change or expressing confusion over the improvement.

- *Reframing:* Also referred to as relabeling, positive interpretation, positive connotation, and reattribution, reframing is an intervention in which the therapist offers a different (typically, nonblaming and positive) view of the presenting problem that enables the family members to think and behave differently within the new context.

- *Prescribing the Symptom:* This is a type of paradoxical intervention in which the client is directed to perform the symptomatic behavior. If the directive is followed, the client demonstrates that the symptom is under voluntary control. If the directive is resisted, the client demonstrates that he or she can give up the symptom.

- *Pretend Techniques:* This is a type of paradoxical interventions in which clients are directed to "pretend" to have a symptom. Because the resulting behavior is the result of pretending, the symptom may be reclassified as voluntary and unreal and thus able to be altered (Goldenberg & Goldenberg, 2000). Madanes (1981) has developed pretend techniques that utilize humor and fantasy, which serve to decrease defiance and resistance.

- *Restraining Changes:* This is a type of paradoxical intervention in which the therapist attempts to discourage the family from moving too fast or even denies the possibility of change.

- *Ordeals:* This is a type of paradoxical intervention in which the family is given a task that makes it more difficult for the family to have the symptom than to give it up.

- *Metaphorical Tasks:* With this type of intervention, directives are given that involve activities or conversations that symbolically relate to the presenting problem and thereby indirectly facilitate change. A well-known example involves having a couple with sexual difficulties describe their preferences for the consumption of an evening meal (which symbolically represents the consummation of a sexual interlude).

- *Devil's Pact:* With this intervention, the therapist asks the family to commit to a task before he or she discloses it. The family is advised that the task is extremely demanding, and therefore they must decide whether or not they really want to resolve the presenting issue.

- *Empowerment:* With this technique, the therapist bolsters family morale and their expectation for change by, for example, informing the family that they must be doing something right or the problem would be worse. The family's sense of failure may be explained as a result of their trying too hard.

- *Using Observers:* An observing therapy team watches the session through a one-way mirror and later offers feedback that is used to influence the treatment process as well as to supervise and train family therapists. Peggy Papp (1983) developed a variant of this approach that she called the Greek Chorus in which observers behind the mirror send messages to the family during the session regarding the process in the session and the dilemma of change.

- *Structured Interview:* With this technique, the therapist uses basic information-gathering skills to aid in obtaining a quick assessment and diagnosis of the family system. Both general and direct questioning may help the therapist more clearly understand the relationships in the system.

Role of the Therapist

In strategic family therapy, the therapist is directive, tactical, and warm and is able to negotiate the terms of therapy such that the sessions remain problem focused and in control. Friesen (1985) suggested that the role of the strategic therapist is similar to that of the structural therapist in the following ways:

1. The therapist is an active agent who joins the family in a personal relationship in order to make structural and interactional changes in the family.
2. The therapist must become a real member of the family and be accepted and trusted as an empathic, approachable helper.
3. The therapist needs some distance from the family to ensure objectivity and autonomy.
4. The therapist needs to provide a supportive but challenging therapeutic relationship.
5. The therapist must be capable of intense relating, rapid assessing, and active intervening. This requires the ability to develop a flexible, creative, unpredictable, and engaging therapeutic style.
6. The therapist requires a repertoire of techniques and a knowledge of timing. He or she needs to know how to adjust intensity and to regulate pressure and involvement.
7. The therapist must learn to use self as the most important instrument of intervention.
8. Resistance is resolved through the relationship, including use of personal charisma, knowledge, influence, and strength. (p. 13)

Haley (1987) stressed the importance of the therapist assuming a neutral stance when working with the family system:

At the most general level, therapists should not side consistently with anyone in the family against anyone else. But that does not mean they should not temporarily side with one against another, because that is in fact the only way therapists can induce change. If they only place their "weight" in coalitions equally, they will continue the sequence as it was. In the same way, if they only join one person against another, they may maintain the system as it was by simply becoming part of the deadlocked struggle. That task is more complex: the therapist must temporarily join in different coalitions while ultimately not siding with anyone against anyone. (p. 126)

Evaluation of the Strategic Family Therapy Model

Brown and Christensen (1986) noted that research in strategic family therapy has demonstrated more scientific vigor when compared to research in other models. Gurman and Kniskern (1981) provided an extensive list of studies that describe different presenting problems to which strategic family therapy has been applied, including schizophrenia, anxiety, depression, delinquency, behavior problems, tinnitus, stomachaches, and work problems.

Much of the supporting evidence for the efficacy of strategic family therapy is anecdotal. However, some empirical research also supports the effectiveness of strategic family therapy. Although support regarding the efficacy of strategic family therapy has been mixed (Schilson, 1991), numerous studies provide positive findings. A study involving the treatment of delinquents by Alexander and Parsons (1973) compared strategic-oriented family therapy with a client-centered family approach, an eclectic-dynamic family approach, and a no-treatment control group. The strategic model had markedly superior results compared to the other conditions in that recidivism was cut in half. The remaining treatment conditions did not result in significant differences in treatment outcome. A 3-year follow-up study showed that problems were significantly lower for siblings of the subjects receiving the strategic treatment than for siblings of subjects receiving the other treatment conditions. A study by Langsley, Machotka, and Flomenhaft (1971) compared out-patient strategic-like family treatment (i.e., family crisis therapy) with psychiatric hospitalization. Their 18-month follow-up evaluation demonstrated the cost-effectiveness and efficacy of the strategic approach, with results showing that the hospitalization group had over twice the number of hospital days subsequent to those that were part of the hospitalization treatment process and six times the treatment cost. Further, a short-term follow-up study on families that received strategic treatment through the Mental Research Institute for a variety of presenting concerns showed that 40% achieved their goals and 32% were seen as significantly improved (Weakland, Fisch, Watzlawick, & Bodin, 1974).

In a review of the research on strategic family therapy, Gurman and Kniskern (1981) noted:

> A strategic orientation to family therapy either shows (a) substantially better results, or (b) considerable promise, when compared with several other (standard) forms of treatment. This is especially true when issues of cost efficiency are considered. (p. 396)

Nichols and Schwartz (1991) urged caution in generalizing research results on strategic family therapy because empirically rigorous studies of the model are few in number and because strategic family therapy is not a homogeneous approach (i.e., the specific types of treatment strategies utilized in the studies can vary considerably).

Schilson (1991) described the primary challenge inherent in performing sound empirical research on strategic family therapy as being the difficulty of devising research design requirements that are compatible with the scope and function of the therapy process. She added that more research needs to be conducted on this model, particularly regarding the critical components of treatment and the long-term effects.

A variant of the strategic model, brief strategic family therapy (BSFT), is being implemented and researched at the Center for Family Studies at the University of Miami. One aspect of this program, the Family Alliance Project, focuses on the needs of inner-city Hispanic youth with drug and behavioral problems and their families (Robbins & Szapocznik, 2000). This short-term intensive approach, which generally lasts 3 months, attempts to change the social context of families by intervening in multiple systems (e.g., family, school, and community). It involves a combination of elements from structural/strategic family therapy with the theoretical work of Urie Bronfenbrenner and the multisystemic interventions of Scott Henggeler. One study of the project's work found that BSFT had a significantly better treatment outcome than a group counseling intervention (Santisteban et al., 1996). The development of BSFT, including empirical research on the treatment outcomes of this approach, continues at the Center for Family Studies.

References

Alexander, J., & Parsons, B. (1973). Short-term behavioral intervention with delinquent families: Impact on family process and recidivism. *Journal of Abnormal Psychology, 81,* 219–225.

Bateson, G., Jackson, D., Haley, J., & Weakland, J. (1956). Toward a theory of schizophrenia. *Behavioral Science, 1,* 251–264.

Brown, J. H., & Christensen, D. H. (1986). *Family therapy: Theory and practice.* Pacific Grove, CA: Brooks/Cole.

Friesen, J. (1985). *Structural-strategic marriage and family therapy.* New York: Gardner Press.

Goldenberg, I., & Goldenberg, H. (2000). *Family therapy: An overview* (5th ed.). Pacific Grove, CA: Brooks/Cole.

Gurman, A. S., & Kniskern, D. P. (Eds.). (1981). *Handbook of family therapy.* New York: Brunner/Mazel.

Haley, J. (1963). *Strategies of psychotherapy.* New York: Grune & Stratton.

Haley, J. (1973). *Uncommon therapy: The psychiatric techniques of Milton H. Erickson, M.D.* New York: Norton.

Haley, J. (1976). *Problem-solving therapy.* San Francisco: Jossey-Bass.

Haley, J. (1987). *Problem-solving therapy* (2nd ed.). San Francisco: Jossey-Bass.

Hoffman, L. (1981). *Foundation of family therapy.* New York: Basic Books.

Langsley, D., Machotka, P., & Flomenhaft, K. (1971). Avoiding mental hospital admission: A follow-up study. *American Journal of Psychiatry, 127,* 1391–1394.

Madanes, C. (1981). *Strategic family therapy.* San Francisco: Jossey-Bass.

Mohr, D. C. (1995). Negative outcome in psychotherapy: A critical review. *Clinical Psychology: Science and Practice, 2,* 1–27.

Nichols, M. P., & Schwartz, R. C. (1991). *Family therapy: Concepts and methods* (2nd ed.). Boston: Allyn & Bacon.

Papp, P. (1983). *The process of change.* New York: Guilford Press.

Robbins, M. S., & Szapocznik, J. (2000, April). A structural approach to changing the social context of families. *Juvenile Justice Bulletin* [On-line serial]. Available: (http://www.ncjrs.org/html/ojjdp/jjbul 2000_04_3/pag10.html)

Santisteban, D. A., Szapocznik, J., Perez-Vidal, A., Kurtines, W. M., Murray, E. J., & LaPerriere, A. (1996). Engaging behavior problem drug abusing youth and their families into treatment: An investigation of the efficacy of specialized engagement interventions and factors that contribute to differential effectiveness. *Journal of Family Psychology, 10*(1), 35–44.

Schilson, E. A. (1991). Strategic therapy. In A. M. Horne & J. L. Passmore (Eds.), *Family counseling and therapy* (2nd ed., pp. 141–178). Itasca, IL: Peacock.

Thomas, M. B. (1992). *An introduction to marital and family therapy.* New York: Merrill.

Weakland, J., Fisch, R., Watzlawick, P., & Bodin, A. (1974). Brief therapy: Focused problem resolution. *Family Process, 13,* 141–168.

6

Milan Model of Family Systems Therapy

MAJOR THEORISTS: Mara Selvini-Palazzoli,
Luigi Boscolo, Gianfranco Cecchin, and Giuliana Prata

Key Terms:

Circularity
Circular questioning
Family games
Imbroglio
Neutrality
Positive connotation
Prescriptions
Ritual

ypically classified as a type of communication or strategic model, the Milan model of family systems therapy is also referred to as systemic family therapy. Of the varieties of strategic or communication models, the Milan systemic family therapy model remains truest to Gregory Bateson's systemic concepts and methods. Important characteristics of the model are its focus on process (interactional sequences) over structure and its emphasis on the past and the history of family patterns.

Mara Selvini-Palazzoli, a psychiatrist trained in the psychoanalytic treatment of children, founded the Center for Family Studies in Milan in 1967 to address the need for community family therapy as a result of the deinstitutionalization of patients in Italy. By 1971, the Milan associates, composed of psychiatrists including Selvini-Palazzoli, Luigi Boscolo, Gianfranco Cecchin, and Giuliana Prata, had adopted a systemic approach to family research inspired by the work of Gregory Bateson and Jay Haley. Currently two major camps exist in Milan systemic family therapy: The Nuovo Centro Team (including Selvini-Palazzoli and Prata) emphasizes family systems research, and the Centro Team (including Boscolo and Cecchin) emphasizes training.

Historical Influences

Members of the original Milan team were psychoanalytically trained psychiatrists who became frustrated with the minimal results they obtained when using long-term psychoanalytic therapy with severely disturbed patients (e.g., patients with diagnoses of schizophrenia or an eating disorder). In 1971 the Milan team adopted a systemic orientation with the ecosystemic work of Gregory Bateson serving as a conceptual foundation. The team was also influenced by the strategic therapy of Jay Haley, and for a period of time Paul Watzlawick served as a consultant to the group. Ultimately, the Milan team isolated themselves to form a new therapeutic model.

The work of cognitive biologists (e.g., Humberto Maturana and Heinz von Foerster) and constructivists (e.g., Ernst von Glasersfeld) has been described as having an impact on the Milan model (Boscolo, Cecchin, Hoffman, & Penn, 1987). In the United States, the Milan model has been influential in the work of members of the Ackerman Institute for the Family in New York City including Peggy Penn, Joel Bergman, and Lynn Hoffman. The Milan model has developed through time and continues to evolve through ongoing theorizing, research, practice, and training.

Philosophy

The Milan model has a systemic epistemology grounded in the work of Gregory Bateson. In this model the most complex explains the simplest (i.e., circular, triadic hypothesis, rather than linear hypotheses, are generated to account for behavior). The therapists (including the observing or consulting team) and the family make up a therapy system; thus, the barrier between the family system and the therapist is removed. This concept is related to the systemic assumption that client-therapist objectivity is invalid. The presenting problem is recognized as serving a function in the family system.

From the Milan model perspective, patterns of interaction can be passed down through generations, and therefore the history of the family is important. The Centro Team focuses less on the homeostatic process in systems and more on the change process, which it views as more important. Relatively long time periods between sessions are necessary to allow systemic interventions to incubate and have maximal effect.

Cognitive processes (e.g., ideas, beliefs, perceptions, fantasies) are addressed along with behaviors. As noted by Boscolo et al. (1987),

> From the beginning the Milan group took mental artifacts as seriously as behaviors. Their philosophy of change was tied to the notion that families come in with "maps" of what is going on and that the therapist attempts to challenge or shift these "maps." (p. 19)

Theoretical Tenets

- *Cybernetic Circularity:* A Batesonian concept, cybernetic circularity describes the recursive and interconnected nature of living systems (Bateson, 1972). The concept served as the theoretical foundation for the following concepts and practices in the Milan model of systemic family therapy: neutrality, circular questioning, and hypothesizing (Boscolo et al., 1987, p. 10).

- *Significant System:* This term is used to describe the units (i.e., persons or institutions) involved in the attempt to alleviate the presenting problem. The significant system usually includes the treatment center, the family, and the referral source and may include other systems such as schools or the court.

- *Neutrality:* The basic therapeutic stance in the Milan model, neutrality arises out of Bateson's concept of cybernetic circularity. Using this approach, the therapy team does not get caught in family coalitions or alliances. Rather than being "nonpositional," the team is "multipositional" (Boscolo et al., 1987).

- *Positive Connotation:* Developed by the therapist, positive connotation suggests that the symptoms and patterns of the problem are good or positive and serve to maintain homeostasis in the family system.

- *Family Games:* Family games are seen as interactive organizations in the family that have evolved over time. All families have games, but not all games are pathological. A symptom in a family member may be an indicator that someone in the family system is negatively affected by a family game.

- *Counter Games:* The Milan model applies this generic label to therapeutic prescriptions that are designed to substitute new rules in the family game. Counter games alter both the elements of the family game and the family structure (Stanton, 1981).

- *Alliances:* A type of relationship that can occur among family members, alliances may be healthy or pathological. An alliance between a child and a parent against the other parent can be part of the pathological family game. A strong alliance between parents is part of healthy family functioning and may be a treatment goal.

■ *Imbroglio:* Imbroglio is a dyadic phenomenon in which a parent bestows special favors on an offspring as a means of acting out issues the parent has with his or her spouse.

Perspectives on Family Function and Dysfunction

According to the Milan model, patterns of interaction in a family system can become fixed and predictable. Patterns that are dysfunctional can be perpetuated across situations and generations of a family. Dysfunctional families make "epistemological errors" in that they follow an outdated map or view of reality as a guide to appropriate behavior. The games in dysfunctional families are covert.

The Nuovo Centro Team has identified and labeled commonly observed patterns of dysfunction such as dirty games and psychotic games (Selvini-Palazzoli, Cirillo, Selvini, & Sorrention, 1989).

The Milan model places minimal focus on the functioning of healthy families. One may, however, speculate on the characteristics of a functional family by generating characteristics opposite to those of a dysfunctional family. For example, a healthy family would not make significant epistemological errors and would follow a basically accurate "map."

Assessment and Diagnosis

Assessment of family problems is conceptualized within a relational context, and symptoms are viewed as indicative of problems in the family system. The therapy team works to maintain a systemic mind-set when conceptualizing family dynamics through the conscious use of accurate languaging. To that end, the team members try to replace verbal descriptions connoting a linear view (e.g., "the daughter is angry") with language that views the behavior within the systemic context (e.g., "the daughter is angering").

Bateson's concept of cybernctic circularity provides the foundation for the Milan model's use of hypothesizing as an assessment process (Boscolo et al., 1987). The therapy team, in conjunction with the family, formulates hypotheses about the nature of the family's problem. These hypotheses are subjected to ongoing evaluation and revision as more information about the family is amassed. The hypotheses are not judged in terms of being right or wrong; rather, they are evaluated in terms of their usefulness in leading to new information that promotes movement in the family. Information is derived from the family by observing interactions, by observing responses to prescriptions, and by asking questions. The questions address specific issues in the context of the family system (e.g., Why is help being sought? Who most enjoys fighting? What is the motivation for change?).

The treatment team uses a balancing formula to assess the likelihood of success in therapy. If more weight is determined to be on the side that favors change, work continues with the family. If the balance is in favor of maintaining the family game, the family is informed that therapy is not currently indicated or referrals are provided. Even though assessment is an ongoing process throughout the treatment period, the first three sessions are more intentionally diagnostic in nature, while the fourth and any subsequent session(s) have more emphasis on treatment.

Goals of Treatment

An overriding goal for the therapy team is to have the family discover, interrupt, and eventually change the rules of their game (i.e., the relational dynamic underlying the family dysfunction). The family may create a solution to their problem that is different from the therapists' goal. The parental couple is encouraged to strengthen the skills that will enhance their leadership function.

The Nuovo Centro Team attempts to achieve not only symptom alleviation and change in interpersonal processes but also family understanding of the meaning of the symptoms (i.e., the connection between the symptom and the family game). An additional goal is to interrupt the rigid game and force the family to create more flexible ways to relate.

Treatment Process

A hallmark of the Milan systemic family therapy treatment process is the extended time between sessions. Typically, 1 month elapses between sessions to allow prescriptions to have full impact on the family system. The number of sessions averages between 5 and 8, with 12 sessions being near the upper limit.

The treatment process typically follows a standard format, including the following steps.

1. *Telephone Interview:* One team member calls the referring family member to collect pertinent information such as the nature of the problem, its history, and general information about the nuclear and extended family. Typically, just one telephone interview is conducted prior to the initial session.

2. *Pre-session Meeting:* Prior to the first session, team members meet to review the information collected in the telephone interview. Initial hypotheses are formulated to help the team understand the family and plan strategies to be used in interviewing the family during the first session.

3. *Session 1:* In this first direct contact with the family, the therapy team describes the logistics of the therapy sessions (e.g., the use of therapists and an observing therapy team; the use of videotape). The therapy team then splits into two subgroups: the therapists (initially, female and male cotherapists were the norm; currently, a solitary therapist may have direct contact with the family) and the observing team. The therapist(s) interview the family while the observing team observes the process of treatment. Both subgroups focus on interpersonal information from the family that will illuminate the family game. As they do so, they examine the information that is gathered within the context of the working hypotheses that they previously developed. After the interview is completed, a structured break occurs.

   During the break, the therapy subgroups reunite to evaluate and refine their initial hypotheses or new hypotheses that have emerged from the session. From the systemic information that has emerged from the session, they develop a positive connotation and prescription regarding the presenting problem to help the family members see the interconnectedness of their presenting issues from a different perspective.

Following the break, the therapist(s) deliver the positive connotation message to the family. This is called communicating the prescription. A prescription or homework task for the family may then be given dependent upon the particular concerns of the family and the stage of the treatment process. The prescription, if used, is delivered in a concise, simple, and understandable manner. Other interventions may be utilized at this stage of therapy as well (e.g., split-team intervention and invariant prescriptions).

Typically, the first session includes parents, children, extended family, and, potentially, other participants who are involved in the family game (e.g., other professionals, neighbors, friends, baby-sitters, and so forth). The first session may be the only opportunity for the team to obtain information about the broad social context in which the family operates.

From the first contact with the family through the third session, the emphasis is on assessment even though the family is discouraged from directly discussing the presenting symptom. Although continued assessment occurs in subsequent meetings, Session 4 and later sessions have a greater emphasis on change processes.

4. *Session 2:* Only nuclear family members attend the second session. In this meeting, changes in the family are recognized by the therapists and the observing team, and assessment occurs on issues that would have been inappropriate to discuss in the larger group at the first session. Even less time is spent talking about the presenting problem than during the first session.

The second interview has three components:

☐ *Connecting Phase:* Therapists continue to collect information from the family, and the family is taught to observe and recognize any differences.

☐ *Analysis Phase:* Focus is placed upon interactions within the nucleus of the family network.

□ *Testing Phase:* Therapists test the motivation of the family and explore parts of the system that will support a discontinuation of the family game.

5. *Session 3:* Only the parents attend the third session. They are asked questions related to issues handed down from their respective families of origin, their marriage, and their parenting functions. At the conclusion of the third session, if the team continues to view the parents as motivated to change, the couple is given a secret prescription, a set of behaviors to use in the home. The parents are asked to keep a diary of the responses to the prescribed behaviors and bring that record to the next session.

6. *Fourth Through Final Sessions:* The fourth through final sessions focus on two primary issues: reviewing each parent's observations regarding the secret prescription (e.g., how did the children react, how have things changed at home) and responses to additional prescriptions provided by the therapy team.

Techniques

■ *Circular Questioning:* With this interviewing technique, developed out of Bateson's concept of cybernetic circularity, the therapists ask one family member to comment on or speculate about other family members' beliefs, feelings, and behavior. Examples of circular questions are:

　　　□ If your sister were to get married, who would miss her the most?
　　　□ If I ask your father, will he agree with your sister or your mother?
　　　□ John, what do you think has kept your mother from hearing your complaints? (Horne & Passmore, 1991)

Particularly during the assessment phase of treatment (Sessions 1 through 3), circular questions are used to expose the family dynamics and enable the therapy team to develop, test, and refine provisional hypotheses. The process of questioning from the therapists also engenders a process in the family wherein they begin to question their own processes in a different way, which makes solution generation possible. Questions relevant to the present issue, relationships in the family, and differences in family members' perceptions are posed.

■ *Hypothesizing:* This process, wherein the therapy team speculates (in advance of the family session) about what may be responsible for maintaining the family's problems, is central to the Milan model. Unless the therapists come to the session prepared with hypotheses to be tested, the risk exists that the family may impose its faulty problem definition and therein prevent solutions. Hypothesizing by the therapy team continues throughout the family's tenure in therapy.

■ *Positive Connotation:* The therapists attribute positive motives to an individual's or family's symptomatic behavior patterns. Terms used to describe a similar process in other models include reframing, noble ascription, and positive attribution. In the Milan model, positive connotation actually denotes more than a technique. It also denotes an attitude shift for the therapists toward a more systemic orientation.

■ *Prescriptions:* With this type of paradoxical intervention, the therapists direct the family or certain members of the family to perform the symptomatic behavior. If the clients follow the prescription, they demonstrate that the symptom is under voluntary control; if they resist the directive, they do so by giving up the symptom. Unlike Haley's use of prescriptions, the Milan model does not use prescriptions to arouse defiance and resistance. MacKinnon (1983) noted that by not trying to provoke resistance to change, the Milan model enables the family to discover its own solutions.

■ *Split-Team Intervention:* This is a type of prescription in which the therapy team informs the family that the team members have different opinions or ideas regarding a particular family dynamic. Hearing all sides of the issue allows the family game to be uncovered, gives the therapists in the session leverage (e.g., we tend to believe the family's explanation), and allows the family to find their own resolution. An example of a split-team intervention would be to tell (or write a letter to) the family: "Half the therapy team sees father as showing his caring for the family when he protects daughter from mother; the other half of the team views father's behavior as a way to help mother deal with a daughter who is quite powerful."

■ *Ritual and Ceremony:* Ritual and ceremony are methods of prescription where family members put into action a series of behaviors designed to alter the family game. The therapists spell out the specifics of the prescription in minute detail (i.e., who does what, where, when, how). The following is the specific text for a ritual delivered to a family, as described by Selvini-Palazzoli, Boscolo, Cecchin, & Prata, 1978):

> On even days of the week—Tuesdays, Thursdays, and Saturdays—beginning from tomorrow onwards until the date of the next session and fixing the time between _____ o'clock and _____ o'clock (making sure that the whole family will be at home during this time), whatever Z does (name of patient, followed by a list of his symptomatic behavior) father will decide alone, at his absolute discretion, what to do with Z. Mother will have to behave as if she were not there. On odd days of the week—Mondays, Wednesdays, and Fridays—at the same time, whatever Z may do, mother will have full power to decide what course of action to follow regarding Z. Father will have to behave as if he were not there. On Sundays everyone must behave spontaneously. Each parent, on the days assigned to him or her, must record in a diary any infringement by the partner of the prescription according to which he is expected to behave as if he were not there. (In some cases the job of recording the possible mistakes of one of the parents has been entrusted to a child acting as a recorder or to the patient himself, if he is fit for the task.) (p. 5)

■ *Invariant Prescription:* Selvini-Palazzoli uses this type of prescription with families that have schizophrenic or anorexic children. The intervention is based on the assumption that a common family game occurs in these families wherein the symptomatic child attempts to take sides in a stalemated relationship between the parents (Simon, 1987). Following an initial family interview, the therapists see the parents separately and give them a fixed sequence of directives designed to promote clear and stable boundaries between the generations. The invariant prescription reads as follows (Selvini-Palazzoli, 1986):

> Keep everything about this session absolutely secret at home. Every now and then, start going out in the evenings before dinner. Nobody must be forewarned. Just leave a written note saying, "We'll not be home tonight." If, when you come back, one of your (daughters) inquires where you have been, just answer calmly, "These things concern only the two of us." Moreover, each of you will keep a notebook, carefully hidden and out of the children's reach. In these notebooks each of you, separately, will register the date and describe the verbal and nonverbal behavior of each child, or other family members, which seemed to be connected with the records because it's extremely important that nothing be forgotten or omitted. Next time you will again come alone, with your notebooks, and read aloud what has happened in the meantime. (pp. 341–342)

- *Disappearances:* This term refers to the component of the invariant prescription in which the parents "disappear" from the household and provide the children with minimal information regarding their actions and whereabouts. This technique serves to uncover and alter the family game.

- *Parents as Therapists:* This technique or therapeutic process typically is used in the fourth session, after the parents have proven their commitment to secrecy from their children. The therapists appoint the parents as co-therapists and consequently "have the pathogenic couple transform into one that can 'cure' their child and, in the process, 'cure' themselves by modifying their relational pattern" (Selvini-Palazzoli et al., 1989, p. 236).

- *Counterparadox:* With this technique, the therapists instill a therapeutic double bind in the family system to undo a preexisting family double-bind message. For example, a common counterparadox is to inform the family that even though the therapists are change agents, they do not want to alter what seems to be a workable homeostatic balance in the family and consequently prescribe "no change" for now (Selvini-Palazzoli et al., 1978).

■ *Instigation:* This term is used to describe the phenomenon in which a family member pits someone else against a third party as part of an ongoing interactional process.

Role of the Therapist

In the Milan model, the therapists' role in the therapeutic process occurs on three levels (Selvini-Palazzoli et al., 1989):

■ In Level 1, the therapists avoid getting entangled in the family game and thereby fail to further its dysfunctional, repetitive pattern.

■ In Level 2, the therapists use prescriptions to invite the family to start playing a different game.

■ In Level 3, the therapists unmask the game.

The therapists must remain in control of the therapy process, yet they tend to limit their expert opinion position. Forming a working alliance with the parents of the nuclear family is a critical function of therapy. The therapists obtain information from the nuclear family and from members of the extended system in a focused yet nonconfrontational way. Reactions to questions are noted, and information from questions is integrated into existing notions of family dynamics. With earlier formulations of the Milan systemic family therapy model, the therapy team held a more confrontational position relative to the family system. Currently, a more collaborative stance is espoused by the Nuovo Centro Team. As described by Selvini-Palazzoli et al. (1989):

> A collaborative atmosphere will enhance the family's willingness to listen, which in turn allows the therapist to listen not only with the head but also with the heart. It also lets the therapist feel free to ask the family members for help in understanding their dilemma. When family members see the therapist as someone

who has joined them in seeking a solution to their problem, and has abandoned all reticence in doing so, the all-round emotional atmosphere will undergo a momentous change for the better. (p. 250)

Evaluation of the Milan Systemic Family Therapy Model

The Milan model has been applied to a wide range of presenting concerns, although two types of presenting issues have received particular attention: families with a member with schizophrenia and those with a member with an eating disorder.

A strength of the Milan model is that its application is more consistent with its theory than is true of other strategic models (Goldenberg & Goldenberg, 2000). Similar to other strategic models, much of the supporting evidence is anecdotal (refer to the evaluation of strategic family therapy for an overview of the empirical research on this related model). The Milan model is particularly difficult to evaluate using standard empirical processes because of the extended time between sessions.

References

Bateson, G. (1972). *Steps to an ecology of mind.* New York: Dutton.

Boscolo, L., Ceechin, G., Hoffman, L., & Penn, P. (1987). *Milan systemic family therapy: Conversations in theory and practice.* New York: Basic Books.

Goldenberg, I., & Goldenberg, H. (2000). *Family therapy: An overview* (5th ed.). Pacific Grove, CA: Brooks/Cole.

Horne, A. M., & Passmore, J. L. (1991). *Family counseling and therapy* (3rd ed.). Itasca, IL: Peacock.

MacKinnon, L. (1983). Contrasting strategic and Milan therapies. *Family Process, 22,* 425–440.

Selvini-Palazzoli, M. (1986). Towards a general model of psychotic family games. *Journal of Marital and Family Therapy, 12,* 339–349.

Selvini-Palazzoli, M., Boscolo, L., Cecchin, G. F., & Prata, G. (1978). *Paradox and counterparadox: A new model in the therapy of the family in schizophrenic transaction.* New York: Jason Aronson.

Selvini-Palazzoli, M., Cirillo, S., Selvini, M., & Sorrention, A. M. (1989). *Family games: General models of psychotic processes in the family.* New York: Norton.

Simon, R. (1987). Goodbye paradox, hello invariant prescription: An interview with Mara Selvini-Palazzoli. *The Family Therapy Networker, 11*(5), 16–33.

Stanton, M. D. (1981). Strategic approaches to family therapy. In A. S. Gurman & D. P. Kniskern (Eds.), *Handbook of family therapy* (pp. 361–402). New York: Brunner/Mazel.

7

Adlerian Family Therapy

MAJOR THEORISTS: Alfred Adler, Don Dinkmeyer, and Jon Carlson

Key Terms:

Birth order
Early recollections
Family constellation
Family meetings
Lifestyle
Purposive behavior
Social interest
Striving for significance

nitially developed by Alfred Adler and his student Rudolf Dreikurs, Adlerian family therapy is distinguished from Adlerian family counseling in that Adlerian family therapy involves the therapist seeing the entire family privately whereas Adlerian family counseling emphasizes parent education and prevention of psychopathology. Despite sharing some basic concepts, the processes of Adlerian family therapy and Adlerian family counseling are different. This chapter will focus on Adlerian family therapy.

Adler's work, originally termed "individual psychology," served as a prototype for later models of family therapy including structural, multigenerational, and communications models. Adler acknowledged that his personal experiences when growing up influenced his theory of personality and therapy. As a child, he was sickly and had several brushes with death. Adler felt physically inferior to his younger brother and learned to compensate for those feelings through mastery in other areas. He also acknowledged the jealousy he felt toward his brother, whom he perceived as his mother's favorite. Themes of inferiority and a compensatory striving for significance in a social context pervade theory and practice in individual psychology and Adlerian family therapy.

Adlerian family therapy continues to be promoted and refined by Don Dinkmeyer, Sr., Don Dinkmeyer, Jr., Robert Sherman, Jon Carlson, and others. Numerous professional journals contain work relevant to Adlerian family therapy, particularly *Individual Psychology* and the *Journal of Individual Psychology*.

Historical Influences

In his professional life, Adler split with his former teacher Sigmund Freud over differences regarding fundamental human motives. Adler proceeded to develop his own theory of personality, which had a strong emphasis on family and social influences. As noted in Dinkmeyer and Dinkmeyer (1991), Adler "called his theory Individual Psychology, referring to the essential unity of the person and of all persons within the social system" (p. 384).

Clinics established by Adler in Vienna around 1922 were among the first that provided couples with marriage therapy. When Dreikurs came to Chicago in 1937, he began to promote Adlerian family therapy in the United States. Dreikurs initiated the development of family education centers, which were designed to promote counseling and education of families as well as train Adlerian practitioners. Currently, the North American Society of Adlerian Psychology and the Alfred Adler Institute of Chicago continue to promote individual psychology throughout North America.

Philosophy

Adlerian family therapy posits that both individuals and social systems are holistic and indivisible in nature, that behavior is purposive and interactive, and that the individual seeks significance by belonging within a social system.

The prototypical social system is the family. Humans are inherently social and desire to help one another. The individual's personality unfolds within the context of the family and its interactions.

In the Adlerian family therapy model, perception is subjective, and individuals create meaning from their own experience. However, behavior is always comprehensible when viewed from within the logic of the family's perspective.

Problems in families result from feelings of a lack of worth or acceptance from others in the family. Therefore, treatment is an educative process that involves the entire family and promotes growth and change. Change in family therapy is effected by addressing interactions within the family system. The interpersonal system is the focus of therapy.

Theoretical Tenets

- *Social Context:* All behavior is seen as having social meaning in the family and in society—that is, as having a social context. People are social beings and spend most of their time interacting with others. Belongingness is a requirement for a healthy lifestyle.

- *Social Interest:* This concept refers to the feeling of being a part of humankind, which is considered vital to a healthy life. It requires an active involvement with the lives of others that is governed by equality and mutual respect.

- *Lifestyle:* In Adlerian family therapy, lifestyle refers to the way in which each individual and family creates its own unique manner of living in society. It involves patterns of behavior that are recurring and predictable.

- *Family Constellation:* Family constellation refers to the patterns and themes of interaction that constitute the organization and functioning of the family unit. Factors integral to the concept of family constellation include the following:
  - *Birth order* refers to the ordinal position of each sibling in the family and the meaning that the family attaches to the position (e.g., the oldest child is typified as the achiever).
  - *Sibling rivalry* is a normal process occurring in families that is due to differences among members and the individual's personal striving for superiority.
  - *Gender roles* relate to the expectations of and for males and females as modeled and mandated in the context of the multigenerational family.

- *Individual Uniqueness:* A central tenet of the Adlerian family therapy model is that each individual is unique. People create their individuality through their perceptions of their family and the world. Each person's uniqueness creates a holism that is not shared with other family members.

- *Behavior Is Purposive:* Behavior is goal-directed and is expressed by the family lifestyle. All behavior has the underlying intention of overcoming inferiority and attaining superiority.

- *Striving for Superiority or Significance:* All individuals experience their smallness in the face of the enormity of the world around and beyond them. This smallness is termed "feelings of inferiority" and can cause people to work throughout life for accomplishment and achievement. This striving to be better than we perceive ourselves to be is the essence of the concept of striving for superiority.

Perspectives on Family Function and Dysfunction

From an Adlerian family therapy perspective, a functional family is typified by democratic processes, where the parents are the leaders of the family yet the children provide input relevant to family matters. Family rules are developed through discussion and agreement. Children as young as 2 years of age can begin to participate in this process in a manner compatible with their capabilities. The parents establish natural and logical consequences so that the result of a child's behavior provides corrective feedback.

Functional families promote the growth and development of the family and its members. They value respect for the integrity of the individual as well as the family's cooperative striving for the common good. Dinkmeyer and Carlson (1993) provided this formula for a happy marriage: Marital happiness equals self-esteem, plus social interest, plus a sense of humor and perspective (MH = SE + SI + SH).

A dysfunctional family is characterized by qualities opposite those attributed to a functional family. Specific manifestations vary with the particular family, yet general problems include:

- Power struggles with parents who lack control or exert autocratic leadership

- Poor communication with blaming and little problem resolution

- Discouragement

- Lack of skills

- Self-perpetuating negative feedback loops

A dysfunctional family does not adequately meet the needs of the individual or the family as a whole. If a family system does not instill a sense of worth within a member, that person may seek significance through destructive, dysfunctional means.

Assessment and Diagnosis

An Adlerian family therapist acquires information regarding the family's goals, priorities, patterns of interaction, individual and family lifestyle, and the function the presenting symptom serves in the system. Strengths and resources in the family are also explored and elucidated. Typical questions the therapist attempts to answer in the assessment phase of treatment include the following (Sherman & Dinkmeyer, 1987):

- What does each family member see as the main challenge or issue faced by the family?

- What does each person want to have happen in the family relationship?

- Is the family atmosphere autocratic, democratic, permissive, friendly, or hostile?

- What lifestyles, games, and patterns are revealed in the transactions between people?

Numerous methods can be employed in the assessment process. These methods are explained in the discussion of techniques.

Goals of Treatment

The overall goals of Adlerian family therapy are to promote beneficial change in individual family members and in the family as a whole and to promote an ongoing process of improvement. Specific goals differ for each family; however, general goals may include the following, which were identified by Sherman and Dinkmeyer (1987):

1. Promote new understanding and insight about purposes, goals, and behavior
2. Enhance skills and knowledge in such areas as communication, problem solving, and conflict resolution
3. Increase social interest and positive connections with others
4. Encourage commitment to ongoing growth and change

Sherman and Dinkmeyer (1987) suggested that goals of Adlerian family therapy are attained by change at several levels:

- Perceptions, beliefs, values, and goals

- Place, structure, and organization

- Social interest, feelings, and participation

- Skills and behavior

- Use of power

Treatment Process

The treatment process can be organized into four phases (Sherman & Dinkmeyer, 1987):

1. *Joining and Structuring:* The therapist gains access to the family system and sets the stage for the remainder of the therapeutic process.
2. *Assessment:* Information is gathered, and tentative hypotheses about family dynamics are formulated. Tests, appraisal instruments, genograms, or other standardized devices may be used at this stage. Interpretations are positively framed for the family.
3. *Developing Awareness and Reorientation:* The family gains increased understanding of problems and continues the change process that began when the family initiated therapy.
4. *Commitment and Termination:* Changes achieved in therapy are solidified, and the therapist begins to disengage from the family system.

Techniques

- *Lifestyle Analysis:* Structured informal interviews are conducted to gain important information about influences on individuals or the family. Primary goals, obstacles to goal attainment, and successful or unsuccessful strategies are some of the areas explored.

- *Use of Appraisal Instruments:* While typically used to gather data in the assessment phase, these instruments can be employed at any point in therapy. Common instruments include the Lifestyle Scale, the Marital Inventory, and the Social Interest Index.

- *Therapeutic Questioning:* The therapist begins this process by asking for reasons that explain why the family is seeking counseling and then proceeds, through questioning and other techniques, to examine the family's lifestyle, constellation, and social interest. See the section on assessment and diagnosis for sample questions.

- *Examination of a Typical Day in the Family:* The therapist asks family members to outline in detail daily aspects of their lives. This process reveals much about family structure and functioning.

- *Preparation of a Genogram:* A genogram provides a visual representation of the multigenerational family history and includes information about birth order, patterns of interaction, and family themes.

- *Early Recollections:* In this projective type of assessment technique, the therapist asks family members to recall their earliest recollections. The recollections they produce occur within the context of current situations and, therefore, have relevance to present issues (e.g., worldview, lifestyle, or themes).

- *Tracking:* With this probing technique the therapist asks each family member, in turn, to describe how a specific behavior pattern began. Ultimately each person's role in creating and maintaining the pattern becomes evident.

- *Examination of Marital Relationship:* The therapist focuses on several aspects of the adult relationship, such as cooperation, equality, social interest, and commitment.

- *Family Meetings/Family Council:* The family is encouraged to conduct regularly scheduled democratic meetings with all family members, regardless of age, to address problems and seek solutions. These meetings, called Family Council, are one of the most commonly used techniques.

- *In-Session Tasks:* Structured activities such as psychodrama, role reversals, role rehearsals and family meetings are conducted to facilitate insight of family members.

- *Confrontation:* Referred to by Adler as "spitting in the soup," confrontation involves the constructive identification by the therapist of an individual's or family's motives or goals. Confrontation must be done positively and empathically.

- *Metaphors, Imagery, and Fantasy:* The use of imagery, metaphor, and fantasy can unearth rich sources of indirect family information. The symptomatic behavior itself is a metaphor for the family's dynamics. Therapists can increase their understanding of family issues by attending to analogical meaning expressed in family language and behavior.

Role of the Therapist

The therapist enters the family system as a partner in the change process who believes in the family's ability to grow toward improved functioning. The therapist conveys this mind-set through his or her optimistic and nonjudgmental stance toward the family. Adler's emphasis on the therapist's use of his or her entire self in an empathic manner with the client is evident in the following quote: "We must be able to see with his eyes and listen with his ears" (Adler, 1931, p. 72). In line with the value he placed on the therapist being able to relate to the experience of being in a family, Adler thought it was beneficial but perhaps not necessary for the family therapist to have a spouse and children.

The therapist also provides structure to the therapy sessions, an act that conveys his or her confidence to the family. The educational emphasis of Adlerian family therapy necessitates a therapist role that is quite active as well as versatile and flexible. Dreikurs (1971) encouraged therapists to have the "courage to be imperfect" such that they can be versatile while trusting their reactions and feelings in the family sessions.

Evaluation of the Adlerian Family Therapy Model

Adlerian family therapy is applicable to a wide range of presenting concerns. Strengths of the model are its comprehensive scope and its flexibility of application. A positive quality unique to the Adlerian model is that many of its concepts can be applied both to family therapy and to family counseling, which is specifically designed to have an educational and preventive focus. A relative weakness of the Adlerian family therapy model is the paucity of quantitative research conducted on its effectiveness. The lack of research is due in part to the Adlerian tradition of being suspicious of research based on statistical methods (Mosak, 1979). Instead, Adlerians have favored a qualitative, idiographic (i.e., case method) approach to research. Case studies documenting the effectiveness of Adlerian family therapy can be found in *Individual Psychology* and the *Journal of Individual Psychology*.

The value of this model is supported indirectly by the influence individual psychology and Adlerian family therapy have had on subsequent developments in the helping professions: As noted by Sherman and Dinkmeyer (1987), "Adler's concerns, ideas and methods cut across what today are called structural, strategic, communications, experimental, behavioral, cognitive, multigenerational, and ego psychology approaches to the family" (p. xi).

References

Adler, A. (1931). *What life should mean to you*. Boston: Little, Brown.

Dinkmeyer, D., & Carlson, J. (1993). Adlerian marriage therapy. *Family Journal, 1*(2), 144–149.

Dinkmeyer, D., & Dinkmeyer, J. (1991). Adlerian family therapy. In A. M. Horne & J. L. Passmore (Eds.), *Family counseling and therapy* (pp. 383–401). Itasca, IL: Peacock.

Dreikurs, R. (1971). *Social equality: The challenge of today*. Chicago: Henry Regnery.

Mosak, H. H. (1979). Adlerian psychotherapy. In R. J. Corsini (Ed.), *Current psychotherapies* (pp. 44–94). Itasca, IL: Peacock.

Sherman, R., & Dinkmeyer, D. (1987). *Systems of family therapy: An Adlerian integration*. New York: Brunner/Mazel.

8

Solution-Focused Family Therapy

MAJOR THEORISTS: Steve de Shazer and Insoo Kim Berg

Key Terms:

Complainant
Complaint
Compliment
Customer
Exception
Miracle question
Ranking
Scaling
Solution
Visitor

eveloped by Steve de Shazer and his associates at the Brief Family Therapy Center (BFTC) in Milwaukee, Wisconsin, solution-focused therapy is fundamentally different from most other types of family therapy in that it is not problem focused. Rather, it emphasizes solutions and the solution-building process in families. The BFTC's development of solution-focused therapy is a continual, recursive process consisting of therapy, research, theorizing, and training. The solution-focused family therapy model is sometimes referred to as brief family therapy, and may be considered a third-generation adaptation of communication and strategic therapies.

Historical Influences

Steve de Shazer stated that the work of Milton Erickson served as the primary foundation for solution-focused therapy. Developments in the solution-focused therapy model have extended Erickson's concepts and techniques. In the mid-1970s, de Shazer worked at the Mental Research Institute in Palo Alto, California, and was influenced by the work of its researchers. In the late 1970s, a group of individuals in Milwaukee with de Shazer and Insoo Kim Berg at the nucleus started the Brief Family Therapy Center. Continuous theorizing, practice, and research at the center have led to refinements in solution-focused therapy practice and theory. Additional key individuals in the development and practice of solution-focused therapy include Eve Lipchik, Michele Weiner-Davis, Bill O'Hanlon, and Scott Miller.

Philosophy

The philosophy behind the solution-focused therapy model is based on the idea that change is constant and inevitable. A constructivist epistemology is assumed, with the model positing that reality is co-created by the therapist and the client in the therapeutic conversation. A future orientation is primary in therapy. Minimal emphasis is placed on the past except for what has previously worked. Binary logic (i.e., either/or) is replaced with systemic thinking (i.e., both/and). The emphasis in therapy is on what is possible and changeable rather than what is impossible and intractable.

According to this model, minimal steps are necessary to initiate change, and once this process is started, further changes will be generated by the client (i.e., the "ripple effect" from systems theory). The systemic orientation of the model emphasizes positive feedback (i.e., change-making, morphogenesis-type processes) rather than stability and homeostasis. And the notion of wholism, such that a change in one part of the system will affect other parts and relationships in the system, is emphasized. Solutions to problems are more similar to one another than different from one another despite the diversity of presenting problems. The emphasis in therapy is on action (i.e., doing something), not on insight or affect.

Theoretical Tenets

- *Solutions Are the Problem:* The model posits that the solutions clients currently use to solve the presenting problem are the problem, not the presenting problem itself. An example is when a client uses a certain coping mechanism that proved problematic in the past to solve a current problem. Hence, the model focuses on solutions and competencies rather than problems. Proponents of the model believe that humans have the capacity within themselves to solve their own problems and that the therapist's role is to unveil or amplify nonproblematic patterns. Developing new solutions is the real work in therapy, not addressing the presenting problem.

- *Complaint:* The identified, or presenting, problem is called the "complaint." It is the reason the family came in for therapy.

- *Exception:* In solution-focused therapy, an exception is any period of time in which the complaint does not occur.

- *New Solutions:* These are new ways of handling the complaint. New solutions frequently develop from exceptions.

- *Types of Clients:* Three types of clients are identified in solution-focused therapy:
  - □ *Visitors:* These clients claim they have no overt complaints. Their rationale for being in therapy involves someone telling them to be there. Visitors are complimented for showing up and are given no tasks.
  - □ *Complainants:* These clients expect some solution to the problem through the process of therapy but may not feel a need to change or take part in the solution. Complainants are given observational and thinking tasks.
  - □ *Customers:* These clients want to do something about the complaint. They are given behavioral tasks.

- *Cooperation:* Solution-focused therapy considers clients' cooperation in therapy and their desire for improvement as givens. The therapist promotes cooperation in the relationship by using interventions that correspond with each type of client. The model is collaborative, viewing the family as the expert on their system. The parts of the system must work together for the resolution of complaints to occur.

- *Therapeutic Fit:* Also known as joining, therapeutic fit refers to the therapist's attempt to understand the family and their complaints and to convey that understanding in a nonthreatening, nonjudgmental manner.

- *Differences That Make a Difference:* This phrase is used to describe a class of noncomplaint conditions that may lead to solutions. The therapist listens for exceptions that do not repeat past ineffective solutions and searches for solutions in them.

- *Rapid Resolution:* Proponents of solution-focused therapy believe that a small change in the system is all that is necessary for the change process to begin. Change happens quickly once the process is started.

- *Equifinality:* This term refers to the concept that any problem has multiple solutions, none of which is more correct than another.

- *Meanings Are Negotiable:* In the solution-focused therapy perspective, the family can negotiate and construct new realities based on current experiences. The meanings the family constructs are what is important, because the family members are the experts on the reality of their system. The goal of therapy is for the family to choose meanings that lead to change.

Perspectives on Family Function and Dysfunction

Solution-focused therapy is a nonnormative model; therefore it does not differentiate or characterize functional and dysfunctional families. De Shazer probably would not use the term "dysfunction," but he has noted that problems in families are maintained by families doing more of what they incorrectly believe will rectify the situation. Problems can also be perpetuated through an expectation that things will recur or not change, a self-referential paradox.

Assessment and Diagnosis

Because assessment and diagnosis typically focus on problems and solution-focused therapy is not problem focused, the conventional usage of these terms is not applicable. However, in a process of disciplined observation, the solution-focused therapist closely watches in-session phenomena (e.g., client conceptual frame, exceptions, client status as visitor/ complainant/customer, and client-therapist fit) and then uses the observed patterns to promote solutions.

Goals of Treatment

Solution-focused therapy has the primary goal of addressing the family's presenting concern. Goal attainment is determined by the family's self-report of an improved state of affairs. Frequently goal attainment is assessed on the basis of the family's subjective estimate of improvement. As de Shazer and Molnar (1984) noted:

> If clients perceive a change, then, in terms of their problems (for clinical and perhaps epistemological purposes), there is a change, whether or not there is an observable behavioral change. (Of course, perceptible, behavioral change is good evidence.) (p. 303)

Formation of goals with the family is a crucial component of the solution-focused model and begins in the first session. It is preferable that the goals be specific, measurable, attainable, and challenging. However, de Shazer has reported that approximately two thirds of the families offer vague goals in the first session. Following the family's description of the goal, de Shazer works backwards from this target to promote behaviors compatible with the goal. For example, if a client reported that therapy would be complete when he or she increased socialization, the work in therapy could involve encouraging behaviors that increase socialization in the present.

The process of measuring improvement toward goal attainment is more important than pinpointing the desired outcome state. An accurate measure of improvement allows for clear feedback regarding the efficacy of therapeutic direction and keeps therapy from being too open-ended. Upon attainment of a satisfactory condition relevant to the family's goal (as determined in the dialogue between family and therapist), therapy is terminated.

Treatment Process

The evolution of the treatment process in solution-focused therapy has been guided by Occam's razor: "What can be done with fewer means is done in vain with many." Consequently, the average number of sessions at the BFTC has decreased from six to five as the treatment process has become more efficient. A fundamental tenet of solution-focused therapy is that solutions have more in common with one another than they have differences, regardless of the differences among the presenting complaints. This belief allows for the use of general treatment processes irrespective of the presenting concern. Although the treatment process allows for variation to best fit the particular needs of the family and the style of the therapist, it follows a fairly structured course. A typical first session would be conducted in the following manner:

1. *Opening:* Make introductions, present the therapeutic model to the family, describe the structure of the sessions, begin to develop therapeutic fit.

2. *Statement of Complaint:* Collect specific information from each family member present about the complaints to generate later opportunities for exceptions and solutions. Have the family rank the complaints by prioritizing what should be addressed first, second, and so on. For each complaint, have the family scale the severity from 1 to 10, with 1 representing the problem at the highest level of severity or impact on the family.

3. *Discussion of Exceptions:* The family describes what is happening when the top-ranking complaint is not present. The greater the amount of detailed information collected regarding nonproblematic times, locations, activities, and participants, the greater the flexibility for solution generation will be.

During these first three steps the therapist uses solution language and questions that presuppose change and emphasize exceptions, solutions, and strengths.

Later sessions follow a similar format except that progressively less time is devoted to discussion of the complaint and more time is spent on exceptions and solutions. A typical session would follow this pattern:

1. *Opening:* "What is different now compared to our last session?" Ask about clues (i.e., homework tasks from the previous session).

2. *Exceptions:* Continue to elicit, recognize, discuss, and amplify occasions in which the complaint is nonexistent or diminished. If necessary, reexamine the complaint to generate more opportunities for exceptions.

3. *Scaling:* Have family members scale or rescale the change or complaint. Accentuate any improvements over previous estimates. Process differences among family members. For example, you might say: "Mrs. Jones, your husband noted a change from a 2 to a 6 and you had a change from a 2 to a 3; what is he seeing that you are not seeing?"

4. *Therapeutic Break:* Thirty-five to 40 minutes into the session, have the clients take a 5- to 10-minute break. During the break, develop

compliments (comments) for the family and tasks for the family to work on between sessions.

5. *Compliments:* Acknowledge the family's strengths and praise members for their contributions to the therapeutic process.

6. *Clues or Homework:* Assign specific tasks to members of the family to be completed during the time between sessions.

The time parameters for a typical solution-focused therapy session are structured as follows: 40 minutes with the family; 10-minute consultation break, 10 minutes with the family to deliver the compliments and clues. The therapy team behind the mirror (when used) is conceptualized as being in charge of treatment, not as being merely observers or consultants.

The structured nature of solution-focused therapy has been refined through the use of decision-making models and computer programs that suggest interventions in the treatment process based on the therapist's observations of the family. This output has been called the "central map" of solution-focused therapy by de Shazer (1988). For example, if the family is able to describe exceptions to the complaint that are predictable and controllable, the central map will likely indicate that the therapist should encourage "more of the same" behaviors that are associated with the exceptions.

Techniques

Many of the interventions used in solution-focused therapy originated as an intervention developed at the BFTC for a particular case. When a generalizable intervention is found effective, the BFTC team attempts to replicate it by using it in other appropriate situations. If a pattern of usefulness emerges, the team studies what is going on that makes the intervention useful (de Shazer & Molnar, 1984, p. 297). De Shazer noted that all interventions in solution-focused therapy are similar in that they help clients experience change in behaviors, perceptions, or judgments. The following are interventions commonly used in solution-focused therapy.

■ *Deconstruction:* With this technique, the therapist questions the client's frame of reference regarding the complaint, particularly if the frame of reference is global. By doing so, the therapist helps the client go from general to specific in terms of his or her understanding of the problem. Breaking down the problem into smaller issues may also make the problem appear less overwhelming and easier to deal with or overcome.

■ *Change Talk:* This term refers to dialogue promoted by the therapist to increase the client's experience of change. The therapist gives the client a directive to "do something different" (de Shazer & Molnar, 1984) to encourage another response from the client's repertoire and provide a new way to attack the problem. This directive is intentionally vague so that the client will choose to do something that fits for him or her rather than be instructed to follow a directive that may be outside his or her frame of reference.

■ *Looking for Exceptions:* To explore exceptions, the therapist may ask, "When the problem is not existent or absent, what is different?" This technique requires a shift in thinking and language for both the therapist and the client.

■ *Circular Questions:* This type of questioning is used in a manner similar to that in the Milan approach. Basically, one member of the family is asked to comment on or speculate about other family members' beliefs, feelings, and behavior. The following are examples of circular questions:

   ■ If your sister were to get married, who would miss her the most?
   ■ If I ask your father, will he agree with your sister or your mother?
   ■ John, what do you think has kept your mother from hearing your complaints?

   (Horne & Passmore, 1991, p. 244)

■ *Normalizing:* When clients assume their response is the only logical thing to do and they feel stuck, the therapist may suggest that "a lot of people in your situation would have . . ." (de Shazer & Molnar,

1984, p. 302). By talking in this way, the therapist redefines stability as the most difficult alternative and advocates for change as being the better path toward the desired stability.

- *Tracking:* The therapist gives the client immediate, positive, verbal and nonverbal feedback that provides the sense that the therapist is following what the client is saying and is really listening. The idea is to give the client a sense of empowerment through validation and confirmation of his or her feelings.

- *Using the Clients' Language:* As the relationship between the family and the therapist develops, the therapist adopts a style of speaking that is comfortable for the family and may be unique to that family. Using the clients' language may involve, for example, using nicknames or slang dialog that is personal for the family and may carry significant meaning to the family members. This interaction with the family must be handled with caution, as the family members may see the therapist's intentions as infringing and disrespectful if a mutually respectful relationship has not yet been established.

- *Punctuation:* The therapist emphasizes certain words or ideas that the client reveals to indicate to the client that he or she is listening and understanding the problem or feelings being presented.

- *Note Taking:* The therapist keeps written notes during the session to record the clients' comments and emphasize to the family the importance of their words. The therapist also emphasizes to the family that he or she is learning from them. The therapist is not the expert and must be taught by the family what they think and feel about their situation.

- *Recruiting an Audience:* The therapist asks the family about the "audience" that may have witnessed changes they have made since the start of the therapy. The therapist could ask, "Who else noticed the difference in your behavior and what would they say about the changes you've made?"

- *Coping Questions:* The therapist asks questions to help point out the client's strengths. The therapist asks the client how he or she has coped with the problem until this point. The client responds by listing what he or she has done to cope with the problem and thus points out his or her own strengths.

- *Gossiping:* Co-therapists talk to each other about what they are observing in front of the family to remain connected and to evoke a response from the family. This technique allows the family members to regroup and get a feel for what is happening in the session.

- *Miracle Question:* Miracle questions are used to encourage thought about change, elicit solution-related information, and provide a standard by which to note changes. The miracle question is presented like this: "Suppose that one night, while you were sleeping, there was a miracle and this problem was solved. How would you know? What would be different? How will your husband know without your saying a word to him about it?" (de Shazer, 1988, p. 5).

- *Utilization:* This is a key concept and class of technique derived from Milton Erickson. Conceptually, de Shazer (1985) defined it as "utilizing what the client brings with him (her) to meet his (her) needs in such a way that the client can make a satisfactory life for himself/herself" (p. 6). In terms of interventions, this technique entails using whatever the client does that is effective, good, right, or fun in the development of a solution. For example, if the client has a gift for organizing and classifying, this talent could be utilized in the service of solution development by having the client categorize things that occur when the complaint is not present.

- *Scaling:* With this technique, the family provides numerical ratings regarding the state of affairs in the family for situations involving or not involving the complaint. For example, the therapist may ask each family member, "On a scale of 1 to 10, with 1 being as bad as it could be and 10 being as good as it could be, where do you rate the situation now?" Ongoing scaling used in sessions presupposes change and provides feedback on differences among family members.

- *Session Breaks:* A structured component of the therapy session, the consultation break occurs approximately 40 minutes into the session. The therapist leaves the family and consults with the team (or with himself or herself if a team approach is not used) regarding the com pliments and clues that will be delivered to the family immediately following the break. It has been observed that the break is similar to a trance-inducing experience for the family in that waiting for the therapist increases their receptivity to the messages delivered.

■ *Giving Compliments:* Compliments are statements the therapist delivers to the family following the consultation break regarding positive things he or she or the therapy team see the family doing. The purpose of compliments is to build a "yes set" (de Shazer, 1982) in the clients to promote the acceptance of a therapeutic task. For example, to set the stage for upcoming directives (i.e., clues), the therapist might say, "The team and I are very impressed with the degree of caring you show for your kids by your constant concern."

■ *Session Tasks:* A task is assigned at the conclusion of each therapy session. A clue or homework task typically used at the end of the first session for families that have difficulty identifying exceptions would be presented like this: "Between now and next time we meet, we would like you to observe, so that you can describe to us next time, what happens in your family that you want to continue to have happen" (de Shazer, 1985, p. 137). In the first and subsequent sessions, clues and homework tasks are delivered to clients subsequent to the compliments. The nature of the clue or task is contingent upon the classification of the clients (i.e., complainants receive observation tasks, customers are given behavioral tasks, and visitors are not given tasks) and their individual characteristics that are most likely to promote solutions.

Role of The Therapist

The role of the therapist in solution-focused family therapy is to:

■ Assist the family to uncover and amplify exceptions and solutions to the presenting complaints

■ Promote an atmosphere where change is expected and belief in the family is unequivocal

- Present self as warm, caring, active, and directive

- Terminate therapy as quickly as is warranted clinically

Evaluation of the Solution-Focused Family Therapy Model

Solution-focused therapy is appealing given the current zeitgeist in the health care and insurance fields, because it tends to be brief, pragmatic, and cost-effective. The evaluation of in-session phenomena and therapeutic outcome that is a part of solution-focused therapy is an integral component of the recursive process of therapy, research, and theorizing. The aim of this built-in evaluation is to continue to refine solution-focused therapy such that it becomes more productive and more efficient. As previously noted, this process evaluation has resulted in the average number of sessions at the BFTC decreasing from six to five (de Shazer, 1988).

An example of the process evaluation was provided by de Shazer and Molnar (1984) when they described client response to the first session task intervention:

> Of these, 50 (89%) clients reported something worth continuing had happened (the range was from 1 worthwhile event to 27, most frequently 5 to 7 events were reported), while 6 (11%) said nothing worth continuing had happened. (p. 300)

Outcome research performed at the Brief Family Therapy Center demonstrated the following results:

> Of 69 cases receiving 4 to 10 sessions, 64 clients, or nearly 93 percent, felt they had met or made progress on their treatment goal (about 77 percent of the 64 met the goal, and more than 14 percent made progress). At the 18-month follow-up, of all 164 clients (94 percent of whom had had 10 or fewer sessions), about 51 percent reported the presenting problem was still resolved, while about 34 percent said it was not as bad as when they had initiated therapy. In other words, about 85 percent of the clients reported full or partial success. (Wylie, 1990, pp. 29–30)

The solution-focused family therapy model has been applied successfully to a wide range of presenting concerns including depression, substance abuse, hallucinations, behavioral concerns with children, and marital discord (de Shazer, 1988).

In a review of 15 controlled empirical studies, Gingerich and Eisengart (2000) explored the treatment effectiveness of solution-focused therapy. Across a diversity of presenting concerns and populations (e.g., depressed college students, adolescent offenders, and individuals in physical rehabilitation), results for solution-focused therapy were significantly better than results for no-treatment groups. In addition, the potential cost-effectiveness of the solution-focused therapy approach was supported in a study concerning rates of recidivism for adult offenders (Lindforss & Magnusson, 1997). Acknowledging methodological problems including lack of comparison treatment conditions and lack of standardized implementation of treatment conditions, Gingerich and Eisengart concluded: "Although the current studies fall short of what is needed to establish the efficacy of SFBT [solution-focused brief therapy], they do provide preliminary support for the idea that SFBT may be beneficial to clients" (p. 495).

Criticisms of the solution-focused therapy model include the danger of clients denying or minimizing valid problems due to the therapist's emphasis on solutions and the possibility of the inaccurate assumption that all concerns brought to therapy need to be "solved." (Experiences such as loss cannot be solved but can be explored, experienced, and integrated). Questions have also been raised regarding outcome claims.

A caution regarding the negative effects from therapeutic practice in general was made by Lambert and Cattani-Thompson (1996) in their review of the counseling literature. The authors cited examples from the literature that suggest that negative therapeutic outcome is relatively widespread across a variety of client concerns, theoretical orientations, and modes of service delivery (e.g., individual, group, and family therapy). They estimated the rate of occurrence of negative effects at 0% to 15% of cases. Mohr (1995) asserted that the negative effects of therapy may be due, in part, to therapists underestimating the seriousness of clients' concerns. Given the emphasis that solution-focused therapy places on exceptions and its use of a limited number of sessions, underestimation of client problems may pose a potential concern for therapists using this approach. Empirical research is needed to assess the degree to which this concern is valid for solution-focused therapy.

Solution-focused therapy has also been applied to the process of supervision in marital and family therapy (Fudes, Shilts, & Kim, 1997). Called focused supervision, this approach involves high levels of collaboration and attention by individuals in supervisee and supervisor roles to language and context within supervision sessions. While discussing cases within a solution-focused framework, the supervisor and supervisee continually reflect upon the meaning-making function of dialogue. The case study by Rudes et al., 1997 used recursive frame analysis as a mode of qualitative inquiry into the actual narrative that occurred in one application of focused supervision.

References

de Shazer, S. (1982). *Patterns of brief family therapy: An ecosystemic approach.* New York: Guilford Press.

de Shazer, S. (1985). *Keys to solutions in brief therapy.* New York: Norton.

de Shazer, S. (1988). *Clues: Investigating solutions in brief therapy.* New York: Norton.

de Shazer, S., & Molnar, A. (1984). Four useful interventions in brief family therapy. *Journal of Marital and Family Therapy, 10,* 297–304.

Fudes, J., Shilts, L., & Berg, I. K. (1997). Focused supervision seen through a recursive frame analysis. *Journal of Marital and Family Therapy, 23,* 203–215.

Gingerich, W. J., & Eisengart, S. (2000). Solution-focused brief therapy: A review of the outcome research. *Family Process, 39,* 477–498.

Horne, A. M. & Passmore, J. L. (1991). *Family counseling and therapy* (2nd ed.). Itasca, IL: Peacock.

Lambert, M. J., & Cattani-Thompson, K. (1996). Current findings regarding the effectiveness of counseling: Implications for practice. *Journal of Counseling & Development, 74,* 601–608.

Lindforss, L., & Magnusson, D. (1997). Solution-focused therapy in prison. *Contemporary Family Therapy, 19,* 89–103.

Miller, S., & Berg, I. K. (1995). *Miracle method: A radically new approach to problem drinking.* New York: Norton.

Mohr, D. C. (1995). Negative outcome in psychotherapy: A critical review. *Clinical Psychology: Science and Practice, 2,* 1–27.

Wylie, M. S. (1990). Brief therapy on the couch. *Family Therapy Networker, 14*(2), 26–31.

9

Narrative Family Therapy

Major Theorists: Michael White and David Epston

Key Terms:

Audience
Circulation techniques
Dominant story
Externalizing
Problem-saturated description
Reflecting team
Relative influence
Restorying/Reauthoring
Storying
Unique outcomes

The term "narrative therapy" connotes a general approach to working with individuals and families that uses the metaphor and language associated with the narrative process to help clients understand the problems in their lives, separate from them, and create alternative life stories. Based on social constructivism, narrative models share a belief in the power of language to oppress or liberate and the ability of individuals to "reauthor" their lives through the process of therapeutic conversations. This chapter focuses on narrative family therapy, considered a third-generation model of family therapy, developed by Michael White and David Epston. Although the intricacies of the language and philosophical assumptions underlying narrative family therapy can be daunting, the essence of the approach is captured in this elegant quote from White and Epston (1990): "Persons give meaning to their lives and relationships by storying their experience and . . . in interacting with others in the performance of these stories, they are active in the shaping of their lives and relationships" (p. 143).

While working as a family therapist in the 1970s in Australia, Michael White was influenced by the work of Gregory Bateson, Edward Bruner, and Michel Foucault. His initial work emphasized traditional systems principles in a narrative framework, and he is noted for developing the externalization process in families. His classic work with externalizing enuresis and encopresis brought him widespread recognition in the 1980s. In recent years, he has traveled extensively throughout the world promoting and extending the narrative model. He is currently the director of the Dulwich Centre in Adelaide, South Australia.

David Epston received training at the Universities of Auckland, British Columbia, and Edinburgh and eventually qualified as a social worker and family therapist at Warwick University and the Family Institute in Cardiff, Wales. Since 1977 his work has focused on problems of children, adolescents, and their families. His collaboration with Michael White in the development of narrative family therapy began in 1981. He is currently codirector of the Family Therapy Centre in Auckland, New Zealand, and continues to be involved in publications and training relevant to narrative family therapy.

A Note About Language: Some of the terms used to format the chapters of this book (e.g., wording in the headings, such as assessment and diagnosis and functional and dysfunctional families) are contrary to the language and even the intent of narrative family therapy. White and Epston (1990) touched on the dilemma posed by the limitations of language as it relates to narrative family therapy in the following passage:

> We believe that "therapy" as a term is inadequate to describe the work discussed here. The terms "therapy" and "conversation" are contradictory by definition, and "conversation" goes some way towards challenging the realities constructed by, and the mystification introduced by, the term "therapy". However, we are not entirely satisfied that the term conversation is a sufficient description of an approach to the re-storying of experience, or that this term adequately represents the unique process we describe. (p. 14 footnote)

Given this caveat, readers should note that language conventionally used in discussions of family therapy, although it may be ill-fitting to narrative family therapy, has been employed to organize this chapter in order to maintain consistency with the format used for other models described in this book.

Historical Influences

Parry and Doan (1994) asserted that the historical mode of cognition in humans is "narrative" in nature in that humans traditionally format descriptions of their experience in stories. The following passage expounds upon this idea:

> Our lives are ceaselessly intertwined with narrative, with the stories we tell and hear told, those we dream or imagine or would like to tell, all of which are reworked in the story of our own lives that we narrate to ourselves in an episodic, sometimes semi-conscious, but virtually uninterrupted monologue. We live immersed in narrative, recounting and reassessing the meaning of our past actions, anticipating the outcome of our future projects, situating

> ourselves at the intersection of several stories not yet completed.
> (Brooks, 1984, p. 3)

The oral tradition of transmitting information through storytelling can be found in cultures around the world. These narratives people told formed the myths that allowed individuals and cultures to make sense of their experience. Since the advent of the paradigmatic mode of thought (i.e., logical positivism, thought processes paralleling the scientific method), the narrative mode has been relegated to an inferior status. However, postmodern thought has pointed out the limitations of the paradigmatic mode and has argued for the legitimacy of alternative worldviews. White and Epston (1990) asserted the advantages of the narrative mode as follows:

- [Stories] capture lived time.
- Stories are richer and more complex as an explanatory scheme.
- Stories are inclusive rather than exclusive (exclusive stories ignore events beyond their purview) and enrich events in people's lives.
- Stories are prospective and encourage meaning making. (p. 126–127)

Other worldviews provide historical precedents for certain aspects of narrative family therapy. For example, the constructivist underpinnings of the model are evident in the first lines of the Dhammapada, an anthology of sayings of the Buddha: "We are what we think. All that we are arises with our thoughts. With our thoughts we make the world" (Byrom, 1993, p. 1). The quote from Shakespeare that reads "There is nothing either good or bad but thinking makes it so" (*Hamlet,* 2.2.259) also has constructivist overtones. Michael White stated that feminist theory, anthropology, literary theory, and critical theory have influenced his thinking.

Philosophy

Seen as a product of postmodernism that refutes such modernist notions as objective reality, expert knowledge, and therapist detachment, narrative family therapy is based on social constructivist thought. The roots of modern social constructivism lie in hermeneutics, the branch of philosophy that addresses the process of interpretation. Originally, hermeneutics focused on the interpretation of biblical passages, but it has expanded to encompass the general process of deriving meaning from written and spoken language. Hans-George Gadamer and Paul Ricoeur are sited as influential figures in contemporary hermeneutics (Parry & Doan, 1994)

Michel Foucault, a French philosopher and self-described "historian of thought" (White & Epston, 1990), also influenced the philosophical assumptions underlying narrative family therapy. Foucault asserted that the power of the dominant narrative in a society (i.e., the belief system that maintains the status quo) pervades all aspects of life and subjugates individuals in the society through the "normalizing" power of language. Multiple influences (e.g., political, social, economic, cultural, and environmental) create the dominant narrative into which many individuals are thrown. Frequently, the power or knowledge base of dominant narratives remains unquestioned; consequently, individuals play a role in their own oppression by their unconscious acceptance of the narrative. The deconstructive process used in postmodernism is similar to the therapeutic conversations in narrative family therapy that assist families in liberating themselves from oppressive narratives.

Like many other theorists and practitioners in family therapy, White and Epston (1990) acknowledged the impact of Bateson's work on the development of their model. Bateson's concept of "differences that make a difference" (Bateson, 1972) can be seen in the identification and amplification of unique outcomes in narrative family therapy. The limitations of knowledge and the process of ascribing meaning to events are additional aspects of Bateson's influence on the narrative model. These concepts are articulated by Bateson (1972):

> The understanding we have of, or the meaning we ascribe to, any event is determined and restrained by the receiving context for the event, that is, by the network of premises and presuppositions that constitute our maps of the world. (p. 2)

White and Epston (1990) linked these concepts with the characteristics of narrative family therapy by suggesting that a therapy consistent with a narrative mode of thought would:

- Privilege persons' lived experience, including their perceptions and interpretations

- Be concerned with the particulars of experience rather than with abstractions and theories

- Foster a perception of the world in which change is seen as the norm

- Appreciate multiple perspectives

- Encourage the use of ordinary, poetic, and descriptive language in the telling of experience

- Invite a self-reflective attitude

- Recognize that stories are coproduced and attempt to engender conditions in which individuals become their own privileged authors

Recounting their journey as therapists, Freedman and Combs (1996) described the following influences on their path toward narrative family therapy. Their list hints at the diversity of influences that have affected clinicians who ascribe to this model.

- The Milan team's exploration of patterns of meaning among family members

- Milton Erickson's pragmatism, view of people as resourceful, and focus on the skillful use of language

- Feminist family therapy's examination of the normative sociocultural context that fosters gender-based power differences

- Social constructionism's position that "the beliefs, values, institutions, customs, labels, laws, divisions of labor, and the like that make up our social realities are constructed by the members of a culture as they interact with one another from generation to generation and day to day" (Freedman & Combs, 1996, p. 16)

Theoretical Tenets

■ *Problems:* According to the narrative family therapy model, the person is not the problem, the problem is the problem. Individuals and families influence and are influenced by the problem. The problem is maintained by an oppressive dominant story and by the individuals involved who function as "life support systems" for the problem.

■ *Storying of Experience:* People organize and give meaning to their experiences by engaging in a process of authoring "stories." These stories then serve a constitutive function, in that people shape their lives according to the stories they author. In developing these accounts, people connect specific experiences of events of the past and present and those that they predict will occur in the future in a lineal sequence. These accounts or stories are sometimes referred to as "self-narratives" (White & Epston, 1990, p. 19).

■ *Language:* Personal and family realities are socially constructed and constituted through language. The power of language and its ability to shape reality are key to narrative family therapy, as White and Epston (1990) described in the following passage:

> As this storying of experience is dependent upon language, in accepting this premise we are also proposing that we ascribe meaning to our experience and constitute our lives and relationships through language. When engaging in language, we are not engaging in a neutral activity. (p. 27)

■ *Dominant Story:* Cultures, families, and individuals have dominant stories. For a culture, the dominant story comprises the normative truths that impact and can subjugate or empower individuals and families and their personal narratives. For individuals and families, dominant stories are the guiding metaphors that serve as perceptual lenses through which information is taken in. An individual's dominant story guides which aspects of lived experience the individual will select for the ascription of meaning.

■ *Literary Merit of a Story:* Whereas the paradigmatic mode of thought assigns value according to "truth" or "accuracy" of information, the narrative mode values the credibility of stories. White and Epston (1990) noted that "the narrative mode leads not to certainties, but to varying perspectives" (pp. 78–79).

■ *Power:* The term "power" applies to several different concepts in the narrative therapy model. The power of the dominant narrative can subjugate people and can be used by individuals to subjugate themselves. In addition, narrative family therapy is highly sensitive to the potential for abuse of power in the therapeutic process. Specifically, the danger exists that therapists can subjugate clients because of power differentials in the therapeutic relationship.

■ *Truths:* In the narrative mode, truths are constructed ideas that are accorded a truth status. These beliefs are normalizing in the sense that they become norms around which people shape or constitute their lives. Global truths are replaced with local truths.

■ *Lived Experiences:* The totality of a person's contact with his or her reality is referred to as the person's lived experiences. The stories by which people ascribe meaning to their lived experiences can never capture the totality of their experiences. The conception of lived experience leads to the idea of the relative indeterminancy of all texts (i.e., inherent ambiguity of and diverse interpretations available for any event).

■ *Problem-Saturated Description:* This term is used to describe a family's perception of itself that tends to be dominated by the "problems" and their repercussions to the exclusion of nonproblem aspects of the family's experience. The therapist uses the process of externalizing to assist the family in emancipating themselves from their problem-saturated description.

■ *Performance of Stories:* This term refers to the enactments, or behaviors, that create meaning in stories. Stories are full of gaps that people fill with their imaginations as they perform or witness enactments. With every performance, people reauthor their lives.

■ *Equifinality:* This term refers to the concept that multiple descriptions and outcomes of an event are potentially present, and none is any more correct than another. That is, there are no essential truths.

Perspectives on
Family Function and Dysfunction

Narrative family therapy eschews terms such as functional and dysfunctional, considering them cultural by-products of a "dominant story" that tends to marginalize and exclude individuals (and alternative stories) through diagnosis and classification. Moreover, the notions of an absolute "truth" and a correct way of perceiving the world, which are implied by a diagnosis, are contrary to the postmodern foundation of narrative family therapy. Rather than attempt to fit a family into singular categories such as functional and dysfunctional, narrative family therapy encourages families to examine their own stories—past, present, and future—and has them critique and often rewrite their stories. Value is ascribed to stories that fit with lived experience, promote freedom, and have coherence and lifelikeness.

Although the terms functional and dysfunctional do not fit with the spirit of narrative family therapy, existing family narratives are co-explored by the family and therapist. In addition, families may choose to share or "publish" their story with other families who wrestle with similar problems, which tacitly conveys the idea that people and families may have similarities in terms of the problems with which they struggle and the activities in which they can engage to reclaim their lives.

Assessment and Diagnosis

As implied in the previous section, terms such as assessment and diagnosis would not be utilized in narrative family therapy because they could convey a pejorative and "absolute knowledge" connotation. However, the model does employ an extensive process of examining the impact of the presenting problem on individuals as well as the individuals' influence on the problem. Some components of assessment within the context of narrative family therapy include the following types of questioning processes:

1. *Exploration of the Problem:* The therapist and family explore how the problem has affected the family's life and relationships.

2. *Relative Influence Questioning:* After the problem has been externalized, its influence on the person (or family members) is explored through questions such as "How has this problem tricked you into not believing in yourself?" The person's influence on the problem also is explored. Questions such as "What have you done to outsmart the problem when it has failed to trick you?" are asked.

3. *Exploration of Unique Outcomes:* The therapist asks questions to help the family explore unique outcomes from the past and hypothesize about possible unique outcomes in the future.

4. *Recognition of Unique Outcomes:* Questions are asked to invite the family to investigate new meanings suggested by the recognition of unique outcomes.

5. *Assessment of Literary Merit:* Questions are asked to assist the family in assessing the literary merit of past, present, and future narratives.

Goals of Treatment

The overarching goal of narrative family therapy is to enable families to reauthor their experience in more positive ways. To work toward this end, a number of subgoals are enumerated as follows:

■ Form a collaborative relationship with the family in which the coauthoring of the family's experience is possible.

■ Externalize the "problem" so that it is not nested in an individual or within the family.

■ Engage the family in a process of deconstructing the mechanisms of subjugation by dominant stories.

- Enable families to identify unique outcomes that contradict their dominant stories.

- Help the family identify and generate new stories that accommodate the unique outcomes that have been uncovered and that have a better fit with the lived experience of the family members.

- Foster a sense of personal agency within family members by using an "audience" to acknowledge their success over the problem.

Treatment Process

The treatment process in narrative family therapy involves the formation of a collaborative relationship between the therapist and the family such that problem-saturated stories can be examined and new stories can be co-authored. Although variation in the treatment process may exist given particular circumstances of families, the treatment process generally proceeds as follows:

1. During the initial contact with the family, the therapist establishes rapport and therapeutic fit. The presenting problem is explored in great detail, perhaps initiated by the query, "What brings you in?" O'Hanlon (1994) asserted that collaboration begins with the creation of a mutually acceptable name for the problem. After the problem is personified and oppressive intentions are ascribed to it, a more in-depth examination of how the problem has affected family members' lives and relationships ensues.

2. The relative influence of the reciprocal dynamic between the family members and the problem is explored and mapped. The influence of the problem on the family may be one of domination or oppression. O'Hanlon (1994) stated: "The problem never causes or makes the person or the family to do anything, it only influences, invites, tells, tries to convince, uses tricks, tries to recruit, etc." (p. 26). The influence of the family on the problem is explored through the recognition of unique outcomes, or times when the family is not controlled or dominated by the problem.

3. Externalizing conversations occur in which the personal identity of individual family members is separated from the problem. The use of a special name selected by the family for the problem (e.g., the monster) facilitates the externalization.

4. Unique outcomes are explored, including areas of relationships that are not problem-saturated. Evidence from the past that supports a different perception of family members in relation to the problem is accumulated (O'Hanlon, 1994). Examples of when family members were strong enough to overcome the oppression of the problem are identified.

5. Homework assignments, tasks, and complements are utilized to underscore the family's increased control over the problem and to amplify family members' awareness of unique outcomes. Continued externalization and the ongoing identification of unique outcomes promote the reauthoring process.

6. New stories that account for the unique outcomes are coauthored. They may be used to establish the readiness for change, recruit an audience, or describe changes that have already occurred. Subsequent stories may involve speculation about future developments related to the family's strengths and victories over the problem (O'Hanlon, 1994).

7. Stories that acknowledge the victories the family has earned over the problem are circulated or published. Published accounts may be made available to audiences (i.e., readers), and opportunities may be coordinated for readers to correspond with the published family (White & Epston, 1990).

8. The therapist becomes increasingly decentralized during the therapeutic process and is eventually "discharged" from therapy by the family (Bubenzer, West, & Boughner, 1994). By positively framing the discharge as a "therapeutic break," the therapist empowers the family and keeps the door open for follow-up collaboration as needed.

Techniques

- *Tracking:* In narrative family therapy, tracking refers to the process in which the therapist closely attends to clients as they tell their stories, demonstrating to the clients that they are being heard and validated.

- *Normalizing:* With this technique, the therapist decreases the oppressive and stigmatizing effects of a problem on a family by providing evidence that others grapple with similar challenges.

- *Scaling:* Also used by solution-focused therapists, this technique involves having clients numerically rate some relevant phenomenon. For example, individuals may be asked to rate (on a scale of 1 to 10) the level of courage they had at a time when they were successful in overcoming the problem. This process presupposes change, underscores differences, and uncovers unique outcomes.

- *Deconstruction:* This term refers to the dialogic process in which the problem is dismantled through a reasoned analysis of its credibility. Wylie (1994) described the use of this technique in narrative family therapy as follows: "In his own terms, White 'deconstructs' the dominant authority by taking people's voices very seriously—accepting their validity as hostile forces 'out there'—collaborating with the person to unmask them as the lying scoundrels they are and develop strategies that will undermine their power" (p. 44).

- *Presupposition of Change:* This phrase refers to the therapist's intentional use of language that conveys the inevitability of change. For example, the therapist might say, "Describe the times when you have outwitted Paranoia" rather than, "If you are able to outwit Paranoia . . ."

- *Externalization:* A hallmark of narrative family therapy, externalization is the process of having clients objectify and, at times, personify problems that they experience as oppressive. The process enables families to perceive the problem as the problem, rather than perceiving certain individuals as the problem (i.e., "internalizing the problem"), and therefore decreases unproductive conflict. It also interrupts the habitual "reading and performance" of the problem-saturated story. The process of externalizing the problem serves to decrease blame, foster intrafamily cooperation, promote a sense of hope, and generate new possibilities for creative resolution of problem situations. In addition, it promotes an opening of space for strengths in the storying process of the family.

■ *Adopting the Family's Language:* The therapist attempts to mirror the family's narrative process to foster rapport, understanding, and receptivity to his or her statements.

■ *Metaphors:* The use of language rich in images and metaphors is characteristic of narrative family therapy. The technique includes privileging clients' metaphors, helping clients use metaphors to personify the problem (which serves to distance the person from the problem), and cocreating new metaphors as individuals reauthor their experience. Employing a metaphor to describe his use of metaphors in the therapeutic process, Epston (1994) stated, "I am like a butterfly catcher, waiting for the metaphor to rise up so I can net it and then display it to the clients" (p. 35).

■ *Verbal Questioning:* This technique involves the frequent use of carefully crafted questions that are posed for a variety of reasons including (a) to gain an understanding of clients' lived experience, (b) to explore origins of stories, and (c) to uncover unique outcomes. The resulting dialogic process with clients can occur in a face-to-face encounter or may take place through other interactive media (e.g., phone conversation, written correspondence). White and Epston (1990) provided the following examples of questions that were used with a particular family in narrative family therapy:

> How had they managed to be effective against the problem in this way? How did this reflect on them as people and on their relationships? What personal and relationship attributes were they relying on in these achievements? Did this success give them any ideas about further steps that they might take to reclaim their lives from the problem? What difference would knowing what they now know about themselves make to their future relationship with the problem? (p. 47)

■ *Locating Unique Outcomes:* This term refers to the process of identifying aspects of lived experience (e.g., events, feelings, intentions)
that fall outside the dominant story. Called unique outcomes, these
aspects of experience contradict the problem's effect on individuals'
lives. Different names are given to unique outcomes based on when
the events are or were placed in time:

   □ *Historical unique outcomes* refer to relevant past events.

   □ *Current unique outcomes* refer to relevant current events.

   □ *Future unique outcomes* refer to speculation about future events.
   A process termed "unique possibilities." With this process, family
   members are asked to use their imaginations to project unique
   outcomes into the future as part of the reauthoring process. The
   therapist can initiate this process by asking, for example, "If you
   continue to outsmart the problem, what other positive benefits can
   you foresee?"

■ *Restorying/Reauthoring:* This is the name given to the creative
process wherein a person or the family as a group ascribes new
meanings (that supplant the meanings associated with the previously
held oppressive story) to their lives and relationships within the context of their lived experience. If the family has resisted interpreting
behaviors through the lens of the dominant story, their story is called
a unique redescription.

■ *Notetaking:* During a session, the therapist may take notes on unique
outcomes or "news of differences" to use later in letters to the family.

■ *Using the Audience or Witnessing:* This technique involves engaging
the active involvement of individuals other than the clients into the
clients' therapeutic process. Michael White stated, "So, regardless as
to whether I am meeting with an individual, a couple, or a family, I
am thinking about possible audiences to the unfolding developments
of therapy, and thinking about how this audience might be invited to
play a part in the authentication of the preferred claims that are
emerging in the process of the therapy" (Bubenzer et al., 1994, p. 78).

■ *Documents:* A distinctive characteristic of narrative family therapy
is the extent to which written documents are used in the therapeutic

process. In general these documents are used to facilitate families' processes of reauthoring their experiences in a more positive, congruent fashion. Types of therapeutic documents include letters of invitation, letters of prediction, awards, and certificates. Letters of correspondence between the therapist(s) and family can be used as substitutes for traditional clinical documentation. These letters are different from conventional professional correspondence with regard to intent and style.

■ *Circulation Techniques:* With these techniques, information from previous interviews is shared with other clients experiencing similar problems through such media as audiotapes, videotapes, and copies of written correspondence.

■ *Reflecting Team:* As in some other models of family therapy, a consulting/observing team may be incorporated as part of the therapeutic process in the narrative family therapy approach. The consulting team can be used to witness the clients' reauthoring process and to provide immediate acknowledgment from a community. The team members also assist in the creation of documents to be sent to the family for a variety of strategic purposes, such as to point out disagreement among team members, to restrain the speed of change, to predict relapse, and to support the gains the family has made.

■ *Consultation Break:* Similar to the session break used in the solution-focused and Milan approaches, a break during the narrative family therapy session permits the therapist to consult with the reflecting team and then, following the break, to share the team's comments, compliments, and questions with the family.

Role of the Therapist

The therapist considers himself or herself a nonexpert who works with the family as they review, critique, and eventually rewrite their story. To this end, the therapist working within the narrative family therapy framework establishes a collaborative relationship with the family, asks questions to help the family free itself from oppressive stories, and serves as an advocate or coach when supporting and acknowledging the successes of the family. Furthermore, therapists may serve as correspondents or even "publishers" (see circulation techniques) as they use written narratives to maintain or accentuate gains made in therapy.

In the following passage Freedman and Combs (1996) offered, in an appropriately narrative and self-reflective style, their thoughts about their perceptions of themselves as therapists:

> Instead of seeing ourselves as mechanics who are working to fix a broken machine or ecologists who are trying to understand and influence complex ecosystems, we experience ourselves as interested people—perhaps with an anthropological or biographical or journalistic bent—who are skilled at asking questions to bring forth the knowledge and experience that is carried in the stories of the people we work with. We think of ourselves as members of a subculture in collaborative social interaction with other people to construct new realities. (p. 18)

Evaluation of the Narrative Family Therapy Model

Narrative family therapy has been applied to a wide range of presenting concerns (e.g., anorexia nervosa, behavioral problems, schizophrenia, encopresis), and the literature provides anecdotal support for the effectiveness of the approach. Because an ethnographic approach to research lends itself to this model, publications on narrative family therapy frequently provide case examples to document the therapy process. Indeed, therapists following this approach have used this type of reporting mechanism therapeutically in the form of "success stories" that describe victories families have experienced over problems.

In a review of the research on narrative approaches, Etchison and Kleist (2000) noted that although there has been a high level of interest in narrative therapies, a minimal amount of research has been conducted. The authors cited the incompatibility of narrative therapy and quantitative research as a contributing factor, noting that most of the published research on narrative family therapy is qualitative in nature. The articles they reviewed did, however, support the outcome efficacy of narrative family therapy with diverse presenting concerns (Etchison & Kleist, 2000). In addition, the authors cited research (Coulehan, Friedlander, & Heatherington, 1998) that provides support for some of the process changes consistent with narrative theory. They concluded that the limited breadth of research on narrative approaches precluded statements from being made about the efficacy of narrative therapy with specific problems.

O'Hanlon (1994) cautioned that some therapists, caught up by the popularity of narrative family therapy, may use it as a technique while missing the essence of the approach. He wrote: "Because the technique is relatively easy to learn, therapists might just go around externalizing problems, like earlier family therapists who went around creating paradoxes or reframing people and expecting miracles. Inevitably, many therapists will ignore the heart of narrative therapy, its fierce belief in people's possibilities for change and the profound effects of conversation, language and stories on both therapist and client" (p. 28).

Another criterion by which a model can be evaluated involves the degree to which it compels a profession to examine its practices. In this regard, narrative family therapy has made important contributions to family therapy through its assertion of cogent arguments for certain beliefs and practices (e.g., externalization, "letters" as case notes, taking the therapist out of the expert role) that are rather iconoclastic relative to other models in the discipline. Narrative family therapy provides the profession with an important reminder about the relational politics inherent in the therapeutic process, as Michael White contended in the following passage:

> "I [Michael White] would like to reiterate that I don't believe that
> it is our mission to be wholly complicit in the reproduction of the
> dominant culture, and, at least to an extent, some of the recent
> developments in theory and practice do enable us to step away
> from that position. These developments encourage us to acknowl-
> edge and to question the politics of therapy, to reject therapy as a
> form of the government of persons, and to consider some of the
> power issues that are part of all therapeutic interactions"
> (Bubenzer et al., 1994, p. 75).

References

Bateson, G. (1972). *Steps to an ecology of mind.* New York: Chandler.

Brooks, P. (1984). *Reading for the plot: Design and intention in narrative.* New York: Random House.

Bubenzer, D., West, J., & Boughner, S. (1994). Michael White and the narrative perspective in therapy. *Family Journal: Counseling and Therapy for Couples and Families, 2*(1), 71–83.

Byrom, T. (1993). *Dhammapada: The sayings of the Buddha.* Boston: Shambala.

Coulehan, R., Friedlander, M., & Heatherington, L. (1998). Transforming narratives: A change event in constructivist family therapy. *Family Process, 37,* 17–33.

Epston, D. (1994). Extending the conversation. *Family Therapy Networker, 18*(6), 31–39.

Etchison, M., & Kleist, D. (2000). Review of narrative therapy: Research and utility. *Family Journal, 8*(1), 61–66.

Freedman, J., & Combs, G. (1996). *Narrative therapy: The social construction of preferred realities.* New York: Norton.

O'Hanlon, B. (1994). The third wave. *Family Therapy Networker, 18*(6), 19–29.

Parry, A., & Doan, R. E. (1994). *Story revisions: Narrative therapy in the post modern world.* New York: Guilford.

White, M., & Epston, D. (1990). *Narrative means to therapeutic ends.* New York: Norton.

Wylie, M. S. (1994). Panning for gold. *Family Therapy Networker, 18*(6), 40–48.

10

Integrative Family Therapy

MAJOR THEORIST: William M. Walsh

Key Terms:

Assessment card
Communication checks
Family meetings
Individual personality dynamics
Integrative theory
Therapeutic gossip
Structural wooden blocks

ntegrative family therapy may be considered a second genera tion family therapy model. Developed in 1975, it is one of the first blended models of family therapy. As with most theoretical models, integrative family therapy has changed somewhat since its inception. However, characteristics that were unique to the original model are still in place and differentiate it from other, more recent integrative models. Integrative family therapy is the only name used for the theory.

Educated and trained as a traditional intrapsychic therapist, William Walsh gradually shifted to systemic thinking as he incorporated into his work developing ideas from the new family therapy field. While his introduction to therapy was through the traditional intrapsychic models of counseling, further professional training emphasized both these individual models and concepts and skills from the group therapy movement. This blending of individual and group models led to an interest and immersion in the theories of family therapy. Walsh (1980) summarized his theoretical position as follows:

> It provides for me the most powerful methods for dealing with the human problem situations that I encounter in my professional work. However, I still rely on the concepts of individual personality development in order to understand the complexities of family living. (p. 75)

Historical Influences

Integrative family therapy blends ideas of several major family theorists (principally, Satir, Minuchin, and Adler) into one consistent model. That is, Walsh selected specific ideas and techniques from these models and modified them to fit his philosophy and personality. The model also integrates specific systems concepts with the traditional ideas of individual personality development. A practitioner of the integrative family therapy approach may follow any one of the many intrapsychic models of therapy and combine its concepts with the major propositions and techniques of the systemic component of integrative family therapy.

Integrative family therapy is the only model in the field today that encourages the blending of any intrapsychic model with the four interpersonal dynamics. Most integrative theories blend only one intrapsychic model with systemic components.

Philosophy

The integrative family therapy model views the family as a network of specific interrelated and interdependent parts. Each person and all groupings of individuals in the family are parts of the whole. The family is significantly influenced by aspects of its unique heredity and environment. Each person in the family responds differently to environmental influences.

All behaviors, attitudes, values, and feelings can be either rational (enhancing) or irrational (dysfunctional) to the individual and the family system. The context in which they are expressed is the determining factor, as they do not possess inherent worth. The total situation including gender, race, and cultural variables, must be taken into consideration when an evaluation is made.

All individuals and systems desire homeostasis. As needs arise, tension is produced in the organism. Satisfaction of those needs reduces the tension and returns the system to a more balanced state. When needs are left unsatisfied, the tension remains in the system and the organism must find other ways of returning to the balanced state. Most alternative methods attempt to reduce tension rather than satisfy needs. Integrative family therapy acknowledges the importance of satisfying needs. In integrative family therapy all behaviors of an individual or a system are seen as attempts to preserve and enhance the organism.

Theoretical Tenets

- *Family Structure:* In integrative family therapy, the concept of family structure is a modification of the structural model developed by Salvador Minuchin (1974). The focus is on the three major subunits of the family—marital/adult, parental, and sibling—as well as on the boundaries within and around the unit. The family subunits are described as follows:

☐ *Marital/Adult Subunit:* This dyad is composed of adult family members who are bonded together by emotional, sexual, or economic factors. This subunit is the source of adult need satisfaction in the functional family. In the dysfunctional family, it is frequently the area of conflict, revenge, or avoidance.

☐ *Parental Subunit:* This dyad is the governing body of the family, the source of decision making, goal setting, and nurturance for the entire unit. The parental subunit works best when the adults function as a team.

☐ *Sibling Subunit:* This group is composed of the children of the family. Ideally, interaction with the whole family helps produce responsible and functional adults. In a dysfunctional family, the sibling subunit can be a place of considerable suffering and acting-out behavior. Thus, it is the source of many referrals for family therapy.

■ *Family Boundaries:* Family boundaries, as described by Minuchin (1974), form an integral part of the structure of the family. Clear, diffuse, and rigid boundaries exist between the subunits and individuals of a family as well as between the family and other external systems.

☐ Clear boundaries allow the two-way flow of information and activity.

☐ Diffuse boundaries create overinvolvement or enmeshment.

☐ Rigid boundaries provide maximum protection yet result in isolation and disengagement.

■ *Communication and Perception:* The communication and perception (C/P) tenet of integrative family therapy is a modification of the theory of Virginia Satir (1967) and is based on Barnhill (1979). Satir emphasized communication and perception as a total process, and Barnhill discussed communication and perception as two parts of a process that he called information processing.

□ Communication involves sending a message. Common communication problems include indirect, ambiguous, incomplete, or double messages.

□ Perception has two parts: Listening to the verbal or nonverbal message and understanding the implicit or explicit message. The most common perception problem is defensiveness on the part of the listener.

□ Faulty perception is considered to be a more common dysfunction for families than is miscommunication.

In most cases, a family will need to make changes in their communication/perception process to maximize the fulfillment of functions. By identifying the dysfunctional element of this process—communication or perception—a more accurate treatment strategy is possible.

■ *Role Responsibility Process:* A role is a set of general and specific expectations that are accepted by or ascribed to an individual. A role may involve specific duties that must be performed on a regular schedule, or it may be a general way of behaving with others. Because completion of tasks is essential for a family to fulfill its various functions, appropriate expectations (i.e., role definition) and follow-through are particularly critical characteristics. If expectations are fulfilled, positive emotional, physical, or material consequences follow; when the expectations are not fulfilled, negative consequences follow. (See Figure 10.1.)

■ *Family Theme:* A family theme is defined as any issue (growth producing or counterproductive) that occurs frequently for a family and that absorbs a significant amount of family members' interest and attention. All families have several identifiable major themes. Negative themes generate the initial therapeutic goals for change.

■ *Individual Personality Dynamics:* These are the strategies that an individual uses to organize, understand, and complete the tasks of daily living. The strategies may be overt or covert and are used for personal need satisfaction. Functional dynamics lead to feelings of comfort and well-being; dysfunctional dynamics distort or avoid

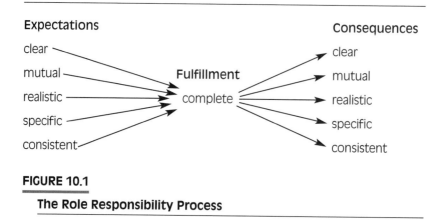

FIGURE 10.1

The Role Responsibility Process

reality in an attempt to attain immediate tension relief. The specific individual model (e.g., rational-emotive, Gestalt, psychodynamic, humanistic) used by the therapist fits his or her philosophy of life. This model is then used to alter an individual's dysfunctional dynamics.

Perspectives on Family Function and Dysfunction

Integrative family therapy considers several tasks that families complete to be considered well-functioning. For example the family traditionally has been the major vehicle for communicating forms of knowledge and skills. The parents and grandparents are the first teachers a child encounters. The learning process is established early, and teaching and learning continues. As children mature in healthy ways, they teach their parents new ideas and new ways of behaving. In this manner, a growth-producing teaching/learning process develops among all family members. The openness and mutuality of this process can be a barometer of a family's health.

When an unhealthy process has occurred for years, the family may no longer be capable of containing the stress and pressure. At this point a professional could enter the picture. The family may seek help on their own, or another societal institution may refer the family for treatment after noticing the family's difficulties. The family may refuse to recognize the problem or to seek professional help. In such instances, the family's problems will likely continue or intensify. Spontaneous recovery is unlikely.

If the family chooses to seek or accept professional help, the therapeutic intervention process begins. Ideally, a professional begins by identifying the dysfunction and then helps the family to make remediative changes. The process may be short- or long-term. Successful intervention results in the family members developing new ways of relating to one another, new problem-solving methods, and a greater understanding of themselves and others. Through therapy, the family learns strategies for addressing and resolving future stress and conflict on their own.

Assessment and Diagnosis

The five characteristics of families described earlier—family structure, communication and perception, role responsibility, family themes, and individual personal dynamics—are used to develop a diagnostic picture of the family. The family unit and each individual within the unit are evaluated with regard to specific and general dynamics. The therapist identifies and isolates the specific problems that brought the family into therapy and translates them into short-term goals for the immediate future. Long-term goals arise from the pervasive, general dysfunction that causes the family pain.

The therapist shares his or her evaluation of the family with the family members, typically during the third session and often in the form of a written assessment card. The assessment is developed based on the theoretical tenets of integrative family therapy, which then become suggested goals of treatment at the beginning of the third session. The assessment card is given to each family member, and the family members state their reactions to the goals listed. Mutual goals are set, and the intervention process begins.

Goals of Treatment

The goals of treatment in integrative family therapy are to remediate specific immediate difficulties and concerns of individuals and the family unit and to build a satisfying problem-solving process that individual members and the family unit can use to deal with future problems.

Treatment Process

Integrative family therapy is a well defined and structured process with a mean duration of 10 sessions per family. It has five specific developmental stages and certain tasks to accomplish at each stage. With the model's organized theoretical process, the therapist has the capacity to impose order, establish goals, and chart future directions.

Stage 1: Structuring   The therapist asserts control from the beginning of the first encounter. The therapeutic relationship is consultative, with the therapist seen as a professional with skills for assisting the family members in finding solutions to their individual and joint problems. By exerting initial control, the therapist instills confidence and optimism in family members regarding the potential for change to occur.

The therapist accomplishes the following tasks during the first session to establish control yet promote an accepting, cooperative atmosphere:

☐ The therapist firmly states the overt parameters of the contractual relationship with the family. The time and length of sessions are discussed.

☐ The therapist encourages all family members to attend the sessions so he or she can observe how they interact, introduce the entire family to the counseling process, and gather information from all family members.

☐ The therapist makes contact with each individual member and elicits help and information from him or her.

☐ The therapist communicates trust, acceptance, confidentiality, and unconditional positive regard to each member to build rapport.

□ The therapist models healthy communication and perception processes. He or she is clear and specific in interactions and insists that family members behave this way also.

□ The therapist teaches and demonstrates the basics of systems thinking to begin the transition from linear to systemic thought processes. This shift from linear to systemic thinking on the part of the family is seen as critical because the absence of systemic conceptualization may be the major reason for premature termination.

Stage 2: Observation and Assessment In this stage the therapist develops a diagnostic picture of family members and the unit as a whole. The various facets of this process are discussed more fully in the assessment and diagnosis section.

Stage 3: Intervention The intervention process, which follows, is based on the assessment stage. Some important aspects of the intervention stage include the following:

□ Presentation and discussion of the assessment card. Each goal on the card is discussed with the family, and examples from previous sessions are used to illustrate each point.

□ The establishment of short-term and long-range goals that determine present and future interventions.

□ The family and the therapist then accept or modify the assessment card. New data are incorporated as therapy progresses.

□ The employment of therapeutic techniques. These techniques are used to move the family through the change process as they address the goals on the assessment card.

Stage 4: Change Maintenance The primary task of change maintenance is to reinforce new behaviors and patterns of interaction. The therapist may continue to employ intervention strategies, but these techniques may be less active and less directive. The family begins taking more responsibility for members' present and future behavior. Time is increased between sessions as the therapist removes himself or herself from a central position in the family.

The assessment of your strengths and weaknesses is based
on observation and clinical evaluation by your therapist.
The assessment will provide important information for you.
A commitment by each member to work on mutually agreed-
upon goals both in the sessions and at home between sessions
will maximize the value of this assessment. Work on each of
the goals will help you and your partner to function more
effectively and help your family to change and grow.

Goals:

1. Helen and Frank need to continue to build their communication skills
   and improve their listening skills.

   a. Maintain eye contact when speaking to each other.
   b. Check to see if you fully understand what the other person is
      expressing.
   c. Practice clear and direct statements by voicing your own needs.

2. Helen and Frank need to make time to talk to each other without dis-
   tractions about their relationship.

3. Helen and Frank need to rebuild trust in their relationship by:

   a. Be honest and clear about your expectations for each other.
   b. Do what you say you're going to do.
   c. Change behaviors in areas where trust has been broken—for exam-
      ple, through secret phone calls and hidden phone bills.

4. Helen and Frank need to continue to work together as a parental team.

5. Helen and Frank need to be consistent with parenting and disciplining
   of their children.

   a. Develop mutual and consistent expectations for the children.
   b. Develop mutual and consistent consequences for the children.

(Walsh, 2001, pp. 38–39)

FIGURE 10.2

Family Assessment Card With Goals—Couple

The assessment of your family's strengths and challenges is based upon observations and clinical evaluation by your therapists in consultation with the supervisory staff. The assessment will provide important information for your family. A commitment by each family member to work on the mutually agreed-upon goals both in session and at home between sessions will maximize the value of the assessment. Work on each of the goals will help your family to function more effectively and help each family member to change and grow.

Strengths:

1. Within their relationship, Janet and Craig have the necessary ingredients for successful parenting: patience, confidence, compassion, and love.
2. Janet has a remarkable personal history of becoming the "champion" in tough battles.
3. Craig's love for Sarah and Janet is genuine as is his motivation to become the best father and husband possible.
4. Sarah is an intelligent, playful, and creative child.
5. The Thompson family has the energy and passion to fuel positive and lasting change.
6. The Thompson family is articulate, outspoken, and interested in what each family member has to say.
7. The Thompson family has a clear understanding of how each family member is unique.

Challenges:

1. Janet and Craig are encouraged to work together as adults and parents in shifting the family picture from an "us" (Craig and Janet) versus "her" (Sarah) picture to one of "us" (Janet, Craig, and Sarah).
2. The Thompson family is encouraged to learn and practice communication skills that include active listening, perception checks, and sending direct messages.
3. Craig and Janet (as parents) are encouraged to identify and develop age-appropriate expectations, rewards, and consequences for Sarah.
4. The Thompson family is encouraged to find a balance between attending to Janet's physical needs and, at the same time, having a family life separate from the illness.
5. Each family member is encouraged to seek support for her or his own individual pains and struggles.

(Becker, 2001, pp. 49–50)

FIGURE 10.3

Family Assessment Card With Strengths and Goals—Family

The therapist assists the family in generalizing its new behaviors and insights.

Stage 5: Termination Termination is indicated when a family displays the following behaviors:

- ☐ Present-day conflicts are resolved in mutually satisfying ways
- ☐ Members express optimism about future plans
- ☐ The family sets realistic goals for the unit and for each individual member
- ☐ Each member has internalized the new behaviors, attitudes, and feelings

    Four-week intervals between sessions during this stage are the norm. The following tasks are included in the termination process:

- ☐ The therapist reviews the family's entire therapy process and specifically reinforces the new behaviors and interactional patterns.
- ☐ The therapist checks each individual's feelings and attitudes toward the changes that have occurred to ensure that each member has personalized and internalized the changes.
- ☐ Future goals for the family unit and for each member are discussed.
- ☐ The therapist presents written and verbal feedback to the family concerning his or her perception of its therapeutic process.

Techniques

Any well-accepted technique from any of the major models of family therapy may be used in integrative family therapy. A sound therapeutic rationale for using a given technique is the guiding principle for the selection of a therapeutic maneuver. The technique must fit the needs and goals of the family to be genuine and productive. The following are examples of common intervention strategies:

- ■ *Tracking:* This term refers to the technique of giving the client immediate, positive, verbal and nonverbal feedback that conveys the sense that the therapist is following what the client is saying and is really listening. The idea is to give the client a sense of empowerment through validation or confirmation of his or her feelings.

■ *Normalizing:* When clients assume their response is the only logical thing to do and they feel stuck, the therapist may suggest that "a lot of people in your situation would have . . ." (de Shazer & Molnar, 1984, p. 302). By talking in this way, the therapist redefines stability as the most difficult alternative and advocates for change as being the better path toward the desired stability.

■ *Assessment Card:* The presentation of the assessment card constitutes the beginning of the intervention stage. Each goal on the card is discussed with the family, and examples from previous sessions are used to illustrate each point.

■ *Enactment:* With this technique, specific problem situations are enacted and discussed, allowing the therapist to assist the family in generating alternative solutions. A therapist may either nondirectively guide or actively manipulate a situation depending on the family's capacities and the theoretical orientation of the therapist.

■ *Therapeutic Gossiping:* Co-therapists talk to each other about something they are observing in front of the family to remain connected and to evoke a response from the family. This technique allows the family members to regroup and get a feel for what is happening in the session (Walsh & Keenan, 2000, pp. 111–120).

■ *Confrontation:* Confrontation techniques may be used to help family members communicate more accurately and effectively with one another. The therapist encourages all family members to openly and directly discuss their perceptions and reactions to situations. An atmosphere of trust and honesty develops, reducing the threat of reprisal or retribution.

■ *Communication Checks:* Communication checks ensure accurate perception on the part of all family members. The therapist establishes a pattern of continually checking his or her perceptions of what has been communicated and encourages the family members to do the same. Through this technique, assumptions and inaccurate perceptions can be quickly identified and corrected.

■ *Roles of the Family:* Working together, the therapist and family define specific roles and expectations for each family member. The therapist encourages all family members to identify both specific expectations they have for one another and specific tasks that are part of each person's role. Negotiation may be necessary to achieve mutually satisfying positions. Consequences may have to be established for the noncompletion of tasks.

■ *Rules of the Family:* The therapist helps the family set general and specific rules that will govern the family members' daily lives. Family members decide how they want to organize their daily living patterns.

■ *Family Meetings:* The therapist encourages clients to hold regular family meetings to supplement the therapeutic contacts. Initially, meetings can be used to practice and reinforce new behaviors learned in therapy. Eventually, meetings can take the place of therapy.

■ *Structural Wooden Blocks:* Children's wooden blocks are used to represent individuals within the family. The blocks are presented to the family as a three dimensional, tactile map that the therapist or family members can move to display different interactions in the family (Walsh, 2002).

Role of the Therapist

The therapist is a professional with specific skills who is employed as a consultant to assist families in finding solutions to problem situations. The relationship is never power-related or adversarial. In a sense, it is a businesslike arrangement that happens to involve intensely personal ideas, feelings, and behaviors.

The therapist controls the therapy session through structuring and instilling confidence and optimism in the family members regarding the potential for change to occur. The family experiences order and stability within the session.

The therapist's behavior provides a model for family members to emulate in the session and in their outside contacts. For example, by modeling healthy communication and perception processes, the therapist teaches the family how to engage in clear and specific interactions. The therapist observes and assesses the family unit and its members to provide feedback to the family and to actively intervene in family patterns.

Evaluation of the Integrative Family Therapy Model

The validity and efficiency of the integrative family therapy model have been tested primarily on the basis of the experiences of therapists and the reports of change by families over a 20-year period. For research purposes, some therapists have completed a rating scale comparing the goals on the assessment card and the final evaluation of the therapist and family to assess the degree of change for major family variables (Walsh, 1991). The five-point scale (1 = no goals attained; 5 = all goals attained) is completed after the final session. Ratings of families seen during the research period range from 2 to 5 with a mean rating of 4.2.

A study by Walsh and Wood (1983) that compared the Dynamics of Family Life Scale, an instrument based on the integrative model, to several other family measurement scales, found the Dynamics of Family Life Scale to be useful in identifying the degree of dysfunction in a family unit. Twenty-six families who were in family treatment because of difficulty with an adolescent member were the subjects of the study. These findings were consistent with the independent assessments of the therapists. In addition, a high degree of consistency was observed between the functional and dysfunctional variables identified in this study and those identified in two major studies of similar instruments (Lewis, Beavers, Gossett, & Austin,

1976; Faunce & Riskin, 1970). The following correspondences were found:

- Functional families typically had a warm and expressive feeling tone, and they were generally more openly expressive and empathic.
- Low levels of conflict characterized healthier families.
- Clear parental coalitions were prevalent in healthy families, and subsystem composition in general was highly related to degree of dysfunction.
- Healthier families tended to be clear in their expressions of feelings and thoughts.
- The relationship between distorted perception and dysfunction was found to be stronger than the relationship between distorted communication and dysfunction.

References

Barnhill, L. R. (1979). Healthy family systems. *Family Coordinator, 28,* 94–100.

Becker, K. (2001). Individual personality dynamics in family assessment and counseling: A case study. *Family Journal, 9,* 48–51.

de Shazer, S., & Molnar, A. (1984). Four useful interventions in brief family therapy. *Journal of Marital and Family Therapy, 10,* 297–304.

Faunce, E., & Riskin, J. (1970). Family interaction scales. *Archives of General Psychiatry, 22,* 504–537.

Lewis, J., Beavers, R., Gossett, J., & Austin, V. (1976). *No single thread.* New York: Brunner/Mazel.

Minuchin, S. (1974). *Families and family therapy.* Cambridge, MA: Harvard University Press.

Satir, V. (1967). *Conjoint family therapy: A guide to theory and technique* (rev. ed.). Palo Alto, CA: Science and Behavior Books.

Walsh, W. M. (1980). A *primer in family therapy.* Springfield, IL: Charles C Thomas.

Walsh, W. M. (1991). *Case studies in family therapy.* Needham Heights, MA: Allyn & Bacon.

Walsh, W. M. (2001). Integrative family therapy for couples. In L. Sperry (Ed.), *Integrative and biopsychosocial therapy* (pp. 17–41). Alexandria, VA: American Counseling Association.

Walsh, W. M. (2002). Working with family structure using wooden blocks. In R. E. Watts (Ed.), *Techniques in marriage and family counseling* (Vol.

2, pp. 71–81). Alexandria, VA: American Counseling Association.

Walsh, W. M., & Keenan, R. (2000). Therapeutic gossip. In R. E. Watts (Ed.), *Techniques in marriage and family counseling* (Vol. 1, pp. 111–120). Alexandria, VA: American Counseling Association.

Walsh, W. M., & McGraw, J. (1992). *The dictionary of family therapy.*

Greeley: University of Northern Colorado.

Walsh, W. M., & Wood, J. 1. (1983). Family assessment: Bridging the gap between theory, research, and practice. *American Mental Health Counselors Journal, 5,* 111–120.

11

Descriptive Summary of Nine Additional Approaches

MAJOR THEORISTS:
James Framo
Carl Whitaker
John Weakland, Paul Watzlawick, Richard Fisch,
    Arthur Bodin, and Carlos Sluzki
Ivan Boszormenyi-Nagy
Samuel Slipp, Jill Savage Scharff, and David Scharff
Harry Goolishian and Harlene Anderson
Leslie S. Greenberg and Susan M. Johnson
Charles M. Borduin and Scott W. Henggeler
Virginia Goldner and Thelma Jean Goodrich

Intergenerational
Family Therapy

James Framo

Having roots in psychoanalytic thought, intergenerational family therapy explores the impact the family of origin has on the marital relationship. Similar to Bowenian family therapy, Framo's work is oriented toward increasing insight and understanding of family dynamics as they relate to unresolved issues passed down from previous generations. This model fits well with couples work, and Framo has used a group model to work with numerous couples simultaneously. Part of the effectiveness of the group approach lies in the vicarious learning that occurs as individuals observe other group members address relational concerns similar to their own.

Symbolic-Experiential
Family Therapy

Carl Whitaker

Whitaker's experience using play therapy with children influenced the development of his model of family therapy. He has also cited the impact of Melanie Mein (psychoanalysis with children), Gregory Bateson, Alan Watts, and Carl Jung on his work. Whitaker's approach tends to be atheoretical, pragmatic, and technically eclectic with a focus on promoting change through a diversity of interventions. Whitaker is famous for using creative and unconventional techniques to challenge or confuse the family. Areas of emphasis in this approach include the experience and expression of emotion in the here and now, promoting the natural growth tendency in families, and recognizing the struggle between autonomy and interpersonal belonging within the family group.

MRI Strategic Family Therapy

John Weakland, Paul Watzlowick, Richard Fisch, Arthur Bodin, and Carlos Sluzki

This family therapy approach originates from the work of a diverse group of pioneers in family therapy (Bateson, Satir, Haley, Jackson, and Weakland) at the MRI in Palo Alto, California. MRI strategic family therapy and de Shazer's solution-focused model are based on a common philosophical foundation. MRI strategic family therapy is strongly systemic in theory and application. The focus is on effective family functioning and adaptability through periods of stress and change.

Contextual Family Therapy

Ivan Boszormenyi-Nagy

This model strives toward integration of a systemic approach with intrapsychic approaches. Its emphasis on the relational context of family functioning extending to many prior generations is evidenced by some of the key terms in this model: rejunctive (behaviors that promote trustworthy relatedness), disjunctive (behaviors that decrease relatedness), legacy (influences passed down from prior generations), and divided loyalty (a pathological alliance of a child with one parent against the other). While emphasis is placed on the importance of relatedness within a family system (with healthy families being fair, flexible, and equitable), the striving of the individual for autonomy within the system is recognized as well.

Object Relations Family Therapy

Samuel Slipp, Jill Savage Scharff, and David Scharff

Based on the work of Freud and later theorists (e.g., Heinz Kohut, Margaret Mahler, W. Ronald Fairbairn, Donald Winnicott), object relations family therapy conceptualizes current relationship difficulties as originating in early child-parent interactions. This model attempts to bridge intrapsychic and interpersonal approaches, utilizing object relations concepts (e.g., individual development, projection, ego identity) within a relations context. The general goal of this model is to provide a therapeutic environment in which the family can understand and resolve unconscious issues that are problematic to current family functioning.

Collaborative Language Systems

Harry Goolishian and Harlene Anderson

Similar to narrative therapy, this model of family therapy is based on constructivism and focuses on how individuals create their experience. The model reverses the typically held position (e.g., characteristics of many first- and second-generation models of family therapy) that the family system causes the problem by positing that the problem promotes the formation of a meaning system (i.e., the family system) around it. Even though a coherent model of collaborative language systems therapy has not been explicated, the process of therapy conceptualizes the therapist as "participant narrative artist" involved with the family in the cocreation of new meanings.

Emotionally Focused Marriage Therapy

Leslie S. Greenberg and Susan M. Johnson

A short-term model of marital therapy intended for moderately distressed couples, emotionally focused marriage therapy integrates intrapsychic and systemic elements. Specifically, emotionally focused marriage therapy utilizes aspects of experiential therapy (i.e., emotional experiencing, meaning-making processes), attachment theory, and systems theory (e.g., focus on relational patterns between partners). These components are operationalized into a coherent nine-step therapeutic process. This therapeutic process strives to promote a reprocessing of partners' emotional responses to each other, therein creating more secure attachments while modifying the partners' patterns of interaction. Emotionally focused marriage therapy stands out among systemic models of marriage and family therapy by having one of the strongest research bases related to treatment effectiveness.

Multisystemic Therapy

Charles M. Borduin and Scott W. Henggeler

Multisystemic therapy is a social-ecological model of family therapy that blends structural and strategic strategies with behavioral and cognitive interventions. Among its distinctive aspects, multisystemic therapy engages of multiple systems (e.g., family, peer, school) in the treatment process, uses empirically validated approaches, and systematically focuses on decreasing barriers to engagement in therapy while simultaneously empowering caregivers (e.g., parents). Its primary application and ongoing development have been with families with adolescents dealing with behavioral, legal, or substance-abuse issues. Despite the challenges posed by these presenting concerns, the outcome literature suggests that multisystemic therapy is quite effective as evidenced by high rates of treatment engagement, retention, and positive therapeutic outcome.

Feminist Family Therapy

Virginia Goldner and Thelma Jean Goodrich

Feminist family therapy is an outgrowth of feminist theory, maintaining as a basis the examination of the effects of stereotypic gender roles on relationships, including issues related to power and communication as they affect overall functioning. The therapeutic process involves an explicit discussion of gender-related ideology as it relates to the presenting problems. Because therapists assume a nonexpert, supportive role, the therapeutic relationship is nonhierarchical. This model privileges women's relational styles and asserts the value of egalitarian relationships. Within the context of feminist thought, couples are empowered to examine and ultimately change their interactional patterns.

Additional Resources

INTERGENERATIONAL FAMILY THERAPY

Framo, J. L. (1982). *Explorations in family and marital therapy: Selected papers of James L. Framo.* New York: Springer.

SYMBOLIC-EXPERIENTIAL FAMILY THERAPY

Whitaker, C. A., & Bumberry, W. M. (1988). *Dancing with the family: A symbolic-experiential approach.* New York: Brunner/Mazel.

Whitaker, C. A., & Keith, D. V. (1981). Symbolic-experiential family therapy. In A. S. Gurman & D. P. Kniskern (Eds.), *Handbook of family therapy* (pp. 187–225). New York: Brunner/Mazel.

MRI STRATEGIC FAMILY THERAPY

Fisch, R., Weakland, J. H., & Segal, L. (1982). *The tactics of change: Doing therapy briefly.* San Francisco: Jossey-Bass.

CONTEXTUAL FAMILY THERAPY

Boszormenyi-Nagy, I. (1987). *Foundations of contextual therapy: Collected papers of Ivan Boszormenyi-Nagy.* New York: Brunner/Mazel.

OBJECT RELATIONS FAMILY THERAPY

Scharff, D. E., & Scharff, J. S. (1987). *Object relations family therapy.* Northvale, NJ: Jason Aronson.

Slipp, S. (1988). *The technique and practice of object relations family therapy.* Northvale, NJ: Jason Aronson.

EMOTIONALLY FOCUSED THERAPY

Greenberg, L. S., & Johnson, S. M. (1986). Emotionally focused couples therapy. In N. S. Jacobson & A. S. Gurman (Eds.), *Clinical handbook of marital therapy* (pp. 253–276). New York: Guilford Press.

Greenberg, L. S., & Johnson, S. M. (1988). *Emotionally focused therapy for couples.* New York: Guilford Press.

Johnson, S. M. (1996). *The practice of emotionally focused marital therapy: Creating connection.* New York: Brunner/Mazel.

MULTISYSTEMIC THERAPY

Henggeler, S. W., Schoenwald, S. K., Borduin, C. M., Rowland, M. D., & Cunningham, P. B. (1998). *Multisystemic treatment of antisocial behavior in children and adolescents.* New York: Guilford Press.

Randall, J., & Henggeler, S. W. (1999). Multisystemic therapy: Changing the social ecologies of youths presenting serious clinical problems and their families. In S. Russ & T. H. Ollendick (Eds.), *Handbook of psychotherapies with children and families* (pp. 405–418). New York: Plenum Press.

FEMINIST FAMILY THERAPY

Goodrich, T. J. (Ed.). (1991). *Women and power: Perspectives for family therapy.* New York: Norton.

Goodrich, T. J., Rampage, C., Ellman, B., & Halstead, K. (1988). *Feminist family therapy: A casebook.* New York: Norton.

Index